Bacchae

Nima Taleghani, after Euripides

methuen | drama

LONDON • NEW YORK • OXFORD • NEW DELHI • SYDNEY

METHUEN DRAMA
Bloomsbury Publishing Plc, 50 Bedford Square, London, WC1B 3DP, UK
Bloomsbury Publishing Inc, 1359 Broadway, New York, NY 10018, USA
Bloomsbury Publishing Ireland, 29 Earlsfort Terrace, Dublin 2,
D02 AY28, Ireland

BLOOMSBURY, METHUEN DRAMA and the Methuen
Drama logo are trademarks of Bloomsbury Publishing Plc.

First published in Great Britain 2025

Copyright © Nima Taleghani, 2025

Nima Taleghani has asserted his right under the Copyright, Designs
and Patents Act, 1988, to be identified as author of this work.

Cover design by National Theatre Graphic Design Studio

Photography (Clare Perkins) by Melanie Lehmann

All rights reserved. No part of this publication may be: i) reproduced or
transmitted in any form, electronic or mechanical, including photocopying,
recording or by means of any information storage or retrieval system without
prior permission in writing from the publishers; or ii) used or reproduced in
any way for the training, development or operation of artificial intelligence (AI)
technologies, including generative AI technologies. The rights holders
expressly reserve this publication from the text and data mining exception as
per Article 4(3) of the Digital Single Market Directive (EU) 2019/790.

Bloomsbury Publishing Plc does not have any control over, or responsibility
for, any third-party websites referred to or in this book. All internet addresses
given in this book were correct at the time of going to press. The author and
publisher regret any inconvenience caused if addresses have changed or sites
have ceased to exist, but can accept no responsibility for any such changes.

No rights in incidental music or songs contained in the work are hereby
granted and performance rights for any performance/presentation
whatsoever must be obtained from the respective copyright owners.

All rights whatsoever in this play are strictly reserved and application
for performance etc. should be made before rehearsals to Independent
Talent Group Ltd., 40 Whitfield Street, London, W1T 2RH, UK.
No performance may be given unless a licence has been obtained.

A catalogue record for this book is available from the British Library.

Library of Congress Control Number: 2025945579

ISBN: PB: 978-1-3505-9260-5
ePDF: 978-1-3505-9261-2
eBook: 978-1-3505-9262-9

Series: Modern Plays

Typeset by Mark Heslington Ltd, Scarborough, North Yorkshire
Printed and bound in Great Britain

For product safety related questions contact
productsafety@bloomsbury.com.

To find out more about our authors and books visit
www.bloomsbury.com and sign up for our newsletters.

Bacchae

**A new play by Nima Taleghani
after Euripides**

The Company

Cast, in alphabetical order

Alexis	**Roman Asde**
Serene	**Melanie-Joyce Bermudez**
Tina	**Natasha Gooden**
Niloo	**Elèna Gyasi**
Clitus	**Sam Jenkins-Shaw**
Bubull	**Reuben Johnson**
Xena	**Kate Ivory Jordan**
Leon	**Tyreke Leslie**
Pentheus	**James McArdle**
Mertha	**Arethajay McEwen**
Nava	**Ellie McKay**
Sunny	**Natasha Magigi**
Vida	**Clare Perkins**
Dionysos	**Ukweli Roach**
Kera	**Anna Russell-Martin**
Yunann	**Ellie-May Sheridan**
Ava	**Fi Silverthorn**
Agave	**Sharon Small**
Tireseus	**Simon Startin**
Rakhz	**Jessey Stol**
Demi	**Amanda Wilkin**

Understudies

Alexis/Clitus/Bubull	**Tyreke Leslie**
Serene/Demi	**Ellie McKay**
Tina/Xena/Mertha/Ava/Rakhz	**Ebony Clarke**
Niloo	**Fi Silverthorn**
Pentheus/Tireseus	**Sam Jenkins-Shaw**
Nava/Kera	**Elèna Gyasi**
Sunny	**Arethajay McEwen**
Yunann	**Natasha Gooden**
Vida	**Natasha Magigi**
Dionysus/Leon	**Roman Asde**
Agave	**Anna Russell-Martin**
Off-Stage Swing	**Ebony Clarke**

Director	**Indhu Rubasingham**
Set and Costume Designer	**Robert Jones**
Choreographer	**Kate Prince**
Lighting Designer	**Oliver Fenwick**
Composer	**DJ Walde**
Sound Designers	**Ben and Max Ringham**
Fight Director	**Kate Waters**
Casting	**Bryony Jarvis-Taylor CDG and Martin Poile CDG**
Voice and Dialect Coach	**Hazel Holder**
Associate Director	**Hannah Hauer-King**
Associate Set and Costume Designer	**Natalie Johnson**
Associate Choreographer	**Ajani Johnson-Goffe**

Opening

Olivier Theatre, 24 September 2025

Special thanks to:

Mumz for joining the PTA and (somehow) convincing them to keep me in school.

Pedz, for every single Tuesday meeting you had to go to.

Haringey Shed for showing me theatre was about community and inclusion.

Miss Franzmann for letting me back into Drama in Year 10 (after kicking me out).

Professor Carol Chillington Rutter for letting me rap my Shakespeare exam.

Alan Lane @ Slung Low for welcoming me to the NFL.

Adam Speers @ ATG for commissioning me, and for being the first.

John MacGregor, Kevin Lin & Max Miller @ CAA for being original believers.

My childhood friend (and barber) Angelos Alexander Milonas for the pronunciations (and trims)

Indhu, for everything. I said I wouldn't f**k it up – hope it was a promise kept.

Jeanie and Sasha – the brains of the business.

And big up all my friends from school, where these rhymes and stories were born.

Bacchae

For Pedz "write it down"

Characters

Dionysos – *god of wine and?*

THE BACCHAE
Vida – *the 'most violent'* **bacchae**
Agave, *Pentheus' mother, royal* **bacchae**
Serene, *young, hyper* **bacchae**
Demi, *brains of the business* **bacchae**
Kera, *next gen, ruthless* **bacchae**
Nava, *hippie, vibey* **bacchae**
Yunann, *has a doctorate in witchcraft* **bacchae**
Niloo, *raw juice cleanse* **bacchae**
Sunny, *wheeler dealer* **bacchae**
Mertha, *erotic fiction writing* **bacchae**
Xena *and* **Tina**, *joined at the hip* **bacchae**
Ava, *got daddy issues* **bacchae**
Rakhz, *dances at inappropriate moments* **bacchae**

THE PALACE
Pentheus, *angry young king of Thebes*
Tireseus, *prophet, all-seeing blind man*
(Bu)Bull, *prisoner, formerly Thebes' greatest warrior*
Alexis, Guard, *oversharer with an intrepid finger*
Clitus, Guard, *'captures' Dionysos in disguise*
Leon the Messenger, *gets eaten alive by Agave. Ouch.*

Note

Dionysos pronunciation (dee-on-knee-zoz) rather than (die-oh-nigh-sis)
Pentheus mispronounces it throughout the play

One

Prologue

Thebes. A bloody white horse gallops from the Mountains towards the Royal Palace.

Dionysos' *Pied Piper anthem gets louder as the horse gets closer. Guards spot it.*

Clitus
It's charging the gate!

Alexis
Archers, attack!

Clitus No no hold fire don't hurt it!! Light the turrets!

Alexis
But it's lost its mind!!

Clitus
Look! It's the Queen's Horse

Alexis
Zeus have mercy . . . why's it soaked in blood?!

Clitus
This means . . . Queen Agave is . . . Hades Hades!

Alexis
The Queen's been killed! The King's mother has been killed!

Clitus
Tell King Pentheus! Hades!

Alexis
Who could have done this?!

6 Bacchae

Two

Vida *interrupts like a boss, addresses audience, set morphs into Mountains.*

Vida
 So melodramatic! Bigman relax with the theatrics!
 Overprojecting ur lines n dat, bruv pipedown n don't chat shit
 Dese peripheral characters need to understand
 Dis is my show! Not even Zeus could steal my thunder fam! Causing such a fuss
 Btw – Agave ain't actually dead – the Queen is now one of us
 Now, I'll excuse u patrons for finking:
 'Why in Zeus' name is the Magnanimous Badgal Vida
 Here in Thebes directly addressing us in our Royal National Theatre?'
 Cos . . . Greek Tragedies kick off with Prophecy & Destiny
 Fate decrees: Tonight I'll lose the boy I raised as my own son
 He'll raise Hell in Thebes den leave u with one hell of a Dramatic Legacy!

Vida *signals to the* **Bacchae**, *who emerge from the shadows.*

 WHO ARE YA WHO ARE YA!

Bacchae *begin choral ritual commemorating arrival, it grows till they have taken over entire stage.*

Bacchae
 We are the Bacchae!
 Bacchae Bacchae Bacchae
 We
 Organise Mobilise Mesmerise
 Hypnotise Feminise Colonise
 We
 Have come to Thebes
 We
 Have come to Baptise

If they resist?
Mystify Mortify Pulverise
Ostracise Terrorise Fossilise!
We do not
Apologise Compromise Westernise
Cos we are the Bacchae
Bacchae Bacchae Bacchae!

Sunny
We dragged the Queen down to earth!

Demi
That horseplay was foreplay!

Bacchae *have now taken over the stage.*

Serene
Yeah! We like to cat fight
I got little clumps n tufts of hair on my fingertips
Cos we be like bitch are you ticklish?
Stick a fingernail through her head's fleshy skin till the
French tip tickles the skull a little bit?

Vida (*aside to* **Serene**)
Chill out u little shit
They ain't ready for all that yet – lemme *hawk tuah* lube
them up a little bit
Eh hem. Hallo. You are Theban mortals, we have so much
in common cos
We . . . are also mortals, but we are from Asia, and we
worship our God Dionysos
He sent us here to Thebes, his loyal followers, we are the
Bacchae
So tonight we'll be your raucous Greek Chorus
We'll have a good old bop, go for a proper gander round
the stage
While our enemies feed you nothing but *propaganda* on
the stage!

Serene
Such a dad joke

Vida (*aside to* **Serene**)
   Quiet. You little ASBO
   So. We are homeless travellers
   We wander from nation to nation
   Granted, your King labels us a Terrorist Organisation
   But really we just topple Dickhead Dictators & provide liberation!

Demi
   I created the DDC: Dickhead Dictator Checklist

Serene
   Every suffering woman's daydream

Demi
   We're like OFSTED . . . for authoritarian regimes

Vida
   Here in Thebes, your King Pentheus comes from a long lineage of kings

Serene
   We had no beef with his predecessors

Vida
   But Pentheus' rule has taken a turn for the . . . stupendously oppressive

Serene
   Women have to be submissive

Nava
   And not in the fun kinda way

Vida (*to a woman in audience*)
   Don't act shy I see u badgal, you got Helen of Troy roleplay
   written all over your face babes
   Women of Thebes u ain't gotta hide ur desires for a threesome or submit to a man's chiefdom!

Bacchae
   Woman Life Freedom!

Vida
See we wouldn't have embarked all dis way if it was just some fight for equal rights shit

Serene
That's light shit!

Vida
We ain't suffragettes fighting for a vote

Serene
We're the big guns!

Vida
Theban women suspected of infidelity get hung up by a rope

Serene
That's why *we've* come!

Vida
By Pentheus' Morality Police, who roam streets, looking for happy women

Serene
Chatty women

Demi
Too much make-up or laughter and his feds cuff n clap you women

Vida
So we're here to free you women by gently imposing Bacchic Rule in Thebes

Serene
By any bloodfire mothafuckin tit-suckin means necessary!

Vida
Don't say that shit I'm tryna act all friendly to dem they're gonna think we're hella scary!
Bacchic rule is freedom, bliss, delicious ecstasy

Demi
We like to touch fuck cum suck

Xena and Tina
Lick spit slurp drip

Demi
Squirt a river make Poseidon proud

Niloo
Drink wine till our eyes is blind

Serene
It drowns the pain so nicely

Demi
Bacchae Freedom's so contagious

Vida
Soon all you Greeks will wanna taste our flavours

Serene
schlup schlup
That's the sound of you sucking extra virgin olive oil out my extra virgin anus!

Kera
I know u wealthy chaps like ur healthy fats

Vida
Men like ur King fink women were made to be their playthings
But bitch I don't know what game ur King finks he's playing?

Demi
Pentheus thinks it's okay to hate bitches

Serene
Put a bitch in her place if u can't placate u may domesticate bitches!

Vida
But we dem *dis-ain't-what-u-quite-expected-from-the-retelling-of-a-classical-play-bitches!*

Now, we shall introduce ourselves individually, eloquently
& succinctly

Serene

I'm Serene, Dionysos' favourite, that's the lowdown
And fun fact bout me – I chopped the left bollock off a
touchy-feely priest in my hometown!

Demi

I'm Demi, Brains of the Business, I created the DDC
strategy!
I scout dictators & discern whether they require light
intimidation or *slice!* decapitation
Basically the glamorous administrator *not* the intimidator!
I leave dat to girls like –

Kera (*deadly serious*)

I'm Kera, Dionysos has blessed me with this Destiny
I'll make every mortal man pay for the sins of their male
ancestry

Vida

Yeah dis one is a fanatical fundamentalist
Yunann, please offset her extremism with a nice joke or
summin about being a dentist

Yunann

I'm Yunann. Hello everyone. I'm actually not a dentist.
Strictly speaking my doctor –

Vida

Yeah yeah ur a doctor rudegirl, science is fascinating, but
let's not bore dem to death, next!

Mertha

I'm Mertha, totally here for the blood & murder
But mainly market research for my Erotic Fiction

Vida

Thank you! Niloo?

Niloo
> I'm Niloo, I was in a child labour camp cos I got caught stealing
> But now I offer raw juice cleanses to women who need healing

Vida
> A very inspiring trajectory Niloo

Nava
> Hiyaaa I'm Nava, relatively new recruuuuit
> And I'm just here to have a jocular tranquil harmonious vibey time with all yous!

Vida
> I said us girlies taking over a Greek Island she thought I meant bar hopping in Corfu!
> Ava, be my guest?

Ava
> I'm Ava, I never knew my father –

Vida
> Daddy issues, we get it, next!

Sunny
> I'm Sunny
> I Fuck Bitches Get Money . . . (by selling teeth, human or animal)

Vida
> Rakhz!

Beat as she gets ready.

Vida
> Too late, lost ur chance, next!

Xena
> I'm Xena

Tina
> I'm Tina

Xena
　And we are

Xena and Tina
　Identical Twins!

Awkward moment.

Vida
　Sure you are

Xena and Tina
　Yes we are

Vida
　And me? Well back in the day, when I was a one-man-gal
　Yeah, believe it or not I was magnanimous

Serene (*sniggers*)
　U mean monogamous?

Vida
　Speak again and I'll recycle u, you know my reputation!

Yunann
　The way Vida sliced her husband's face off with his own razor u'd think she was changing
　The feng shui the way she gave his face a rearranging

Vida
　I chose maroon, crimson and scarlet for his face's redecoration.

Serene
　That what you meant by act friendly?

Vida
　What?!!! The man tried to rob my oesophagus of its oxygen
　Anyway, Zeus himself delivered his very own son, newborn baby Dionysos to *me*
　I raised Dio like we shared an umbilical from a minuscule little youth

To a lyrical, multi-syllable rhyming miracle!
Now we're back where Dio was born, this shit is full circle!

Serene

Spherical!

Vida

It's showtime!
And right on cue introducing: Uncle Prehistorical!

Yunann

Tireseus the blind prophet

Demi

Famous throughout Greece for being a clairvoyant oracle

Yunann

He's here to have a word with Pentheus' Palace Guard

Demi

Little Alexis, he may be loyal to Pentheus but he really does have a heart

Three

Palace.

Tireseus

I require an imminent audience with Pentheus

Alexis

Respectfully sir, to your stature and pedigree
I'm afraid I can't permit you entry, presently

Tireseus

Alexis, it's a matter of utmost importance to be handled discreetly and delicately

Alexis

It must wait

Tireseus

Why?

Alexis
I *categorically* can't say . . . I mean . . .

Tireseus
. . . yes?

Alexis
You see, the King's mother, Queen Agave . . . is *dead*

Vida *lets out a sarcastic snigger, walks into the shadows.*

So he can't take any more bad news he's in quite a state
There is *certainly* nothing more I can say.

Tireseus
Understood

Alexis
. . . I mean it's brought up old wounds of his daughter's death if you ask me
We know how *different* he became after that

Tireseus
Well it needn't

Alexis
I mean, respectfully sir I'm about to be a father myself the missus is six months up the duff so I'm really starting to empathise with the loss of a child . . . like in a *hypothetical* sense

Tireseus
Congratulations, Alexis

Alexis
Thank you Sir, I'm happy but it's twins you see, so I'm shitting it if I'm being brutally honest –

Tireseus
Alexis, has Agave's body been recovered?

Vida *slowly returns with a shrouded figure.*

Alexis
> No. I mean I shouldn't be telling you this but, her Royal horse returned to the Palace, get this, soaked in her blood ... we even found tufts of the Queen's hair ...

Spotlight on **Serene**, *sprinkling tufts of hair from her fingers, which fall like glitter under the light.*

Tireseus
> What colour is her horse?

Alexis
> Royal White of course

Tireseus
> It is an Omen, young man, Agave is alive, let me in
> I need to urgently warn the King this is his moment of
> Fated Reckoning!
> The God Dionysos, is near

Alexis
> Sir I unequivocally cannot let you in, woh wait, did – did you say the *God*?
> The one they say invented wine? I heard rumours it makes a man feel ... sublime

Tireseus
> Alexis, it inspires a man to speak in rhyme
> And more

Alexis
> How can you be sure?

Tireseus
> I've tried it

Alexis *gasps.*

Tireseus
> Now, the God could arrive at any moment in any number of disguises

Demi (*aside to* **Vida**)
We need to keep an eye on Tireseus, he really ruins surprises

Tireseus
And remember, Alexis, we always have Choice before our Fate is decided

Alexis
I could lose my job I got bills to pay & *babies* on the way! It's a very plural situation sir!

Tireseus
The Bacchae have arrived in the Theban mountains

Bacchae
Surprise!

Tireseus
Therefore, I require an imminent audience with the King

Alexis
Okay, I suppose you should probably tell the king *that* Hades! Wait, this means Queen Agave's been *kidnapped?!*

Four

Mountains

Vida
Kidnapped?! Na! Dionysos sent her to us via Royal Mail delivery!

Vida *presents* **Agave** *as prize capture, chunks of hair missing, open wounds on her head.*

Serene
WE GOT THE MOTHAFUCKIN THEBAN QUEEN ON OUR TEAM BITCH PLEASE!

Kera
Gave her a little clap-slap initiation –

Vida
Turns out she's a tough little Royal Bacchae, isn't she?!

Agave (*surveying the* **Bacchae**)
I've never been amongst so many –

Kera
Boss bitches?

Agave
Er . . . no

Niloo
Pretty Bacchae witches?

Agave
No

Niloo
What den?

Agave
. . . *common people*

Serene
Bitch how u still on ur high horse?!

Vida
Chill Serene, u gotta remember you're chatting to a Queen
See, you lot, Agave here, and her sister Semele –

Agave
Semele shamed our family

Vida
Were both raised to be
Distinguished stinking-rich princesses of the highest
Theban pedigree

Agave
This is Ancient Greek history

Vida (*smiling*)
Which is exactly what these discerning patrons have paid to see
Agave you had one son and one son alone

Demi
>Pentheus the Prick who today sits on the throne

Agave
>Don't you talk like that about my Pen Pen!

Vida
>But Semele . . . well she happened to have a son of her *own*

Serene
>SHE FUCKED ZEUS!!

Vida
>YO!

Agave
>No!

Serene
>What? I was just excited for them to know!

Vida
>Why can't you never let a story just flow
>You always sabotage punchlines
>We're trying to put on a bloody show!

Serene
>I don't sabotage punchlines

Vida
>What about in Syria . . . ?

Serene
>That was one time!!!

Demi (*aside*)
>We do not air our dirty laundry out in public!

Vida
>As I was saying
>Before I was so cruelly interrupted:
>Yes the headline news
>Was that slim Semele
>Had only gone and fucked Zeus

Agave
In her dreams! Zeus was after me!

Vida *looks around,* **Bacchae** *queue up to be picked.*

Vida
Zeus'll be played by . . .

Demi
Nava!

Nava
I genuinely find it *offensive* and super *problematic* to even *pretend* to be *such* a misogy –

Vida
Dis is theatre fam, we can't all be goodies otherwise there's no story, so:
Save ur opinions for ur podcast, do a coupla tongue twisters, and get in *character!!!*

Nava *reluctantly 'becomes'* **Zeus**, *as the others raise hands again.*

Semele will be played by . . . Kera

Kera
An oppressed woman I identify with? Happily

Kera *becomes* **Semele**.

Semele
Hey . . . I'm Semele, and yes, Zeus got me pregnant

Demi
See Zeus can be so charming, like:

Zeus
You are just my type

Demi
He seduces by throwing two bolts at once, like

Zeus
Have u ever seen lightning strike twice?

Demi
But his most common mode is forceful, like:

Zeus
I know you like my Zeusyness
And dat uterus belongs to me now

Vida
But thing is yeah, Zeus had a wife – Hera

Serene *is over the moon to be picked.*

Hera
YES! YESSS! My dream role! I'm Hera mothafuckaz
I ain't a God who's known for being cordial
Or take kindly to my man impregnating a mere mortal

Zeus
These mortal groupies don't mean shit to me – ask Aphrodite boo
I've only got eyes for you!

Semele
Psst Zeus, I'm pregnant with your baby

Zeus
Ohhh shit, how long down the line are you?

Semele
Six months

Hera
She's six months preggers?!

Zeus
Understandably . . . you're jealous.

Vida
A kerfuffle ensues
Then the baby is no longer in Semele's belly but

Zeus
I will save you by stitching you inside my thigh, why not, after all, I'm Zeus!

Vida
>Six months in Semele's belly
>Three months in Zeus' thigh
>And lo and behold
>A powerful God grew inside

Demi
>So Dionysos was
>Mothered by his father

Vida
>What a fuckin palaver!

Demi
>As for his unlucky mummy –

Hera
>Semele
>You think you can fuck my man raw
>Right before
>He jumps into bed with me?
>Bitch you are skin and bones
>You fink Zeus wants your dead food
>When he's got steak at home?!

All
>Ummmmmmm!

Semele
>Hera, it's not what it looks like AT ALL!

Hera (*changes tone*)
>U got your skinny self in a situation u ain't thick enough to handle

All
>Mmmmmmm

Hera (*double time*)
>You got yourself pregnant with my man's baby
>I bet this ain't the way she
>Thought she would have her hands full

All
   OOOOHHhhhh

Hera (*softer, slower*)
   You thought you'd have your hands full of *love*
   Instead you'll have your hands full of *blood*
   One bang two bangs three bangs more
   Four bangs

Demi
   She sang

Hera (*operatic*)
   Fam it's warrrrrrrrrr

Hera *starts beating on* **Semele**, **Agave** *watches in horror.*

Agave
   Stop! We don't need to see this!

Hera
   Semele you can't do fuckall
   Look what you made me do, Zeus!

Zeus *looks guilty.*

   Cracked the woman's skull so many times I broke my own knuckle

Vida
   What a fucking knuckle-crushing kerfuffle

Demi
   Hera burnt her alive with Fire

Hera
   I had to teach Zeus a lesson for polluting our covenant
   Rolled his bitch in a spliff n made him smoke her as punishment!

All
   WOW!

Vida
Good job girls, u can de-robe outta character now
(*To audience.*) You're welcome to hire these artists for other historical reenactments:
Battle of Troy, The Abduction of Persephone and the weird one where the King shags his
mum n kills his dad, we charge extra for dat freaky shit tho

Agave (*visibly faint*)
I don't feel very . . .

Niloo (*hands* **Agave** *a bottle of red liquid*)
Drink dis

Agave
What is it?

Niloo
It'll heal your chakra and detox your microbiome, take a sip

Agave *sips gingerly, then takes a glug, then to everyone's shock, downs the whole thing.*

Agave
Uhm what was that?

Niloo
Lion's blood . . . mixed with some other shit

Nava
Gosh girls, I really *went* there . . . really embodied it . . .
Holy shit, what if I'm a closeted misogynist?!

Kera (*deadpan*)
There's nothing Zeus wouldn't do to humiliate a woman
Therefore there's no man I wouldn't castrate, any age, any height, any race

Vida
You're a very over-zealous zealot u know dat, imagine coming home to her after a hard day?

Agave
I lied about Semele
Zeus played us against each other, then he chose her over me

Kera
Would u like redemption, majesty?

Agave
I surely would

Kera
Then worship our God Dionysos rampantly

Agave
You really believe my nephew is a true God . . . of what?

Demi
Wine & rhyme & freeing women one Godforsaken nation at a time

Agave
You're *free* women? Truly?

Serene
Free & Bad & Boujie

Kera
You came here to be free too, didn't you?

Agave (*confused*)
I felt a calling then I was here next thing I knew

Vida
Cos Dionysos sent u an invitation u couldn't refuse
But you knew u raised a proper prick for a son
And, talking of scum!

Xena *and* **Tina**
Something *dickhead* this way comes!

Agave
Don't call my son that, you've no idea the torment he's been through
He lost his little girl, my beloved granddaughter

Mertha
Tireseus has finally got to the Prick Pentheus

Nava
Think Pentheus'll welcome our arrival in Thebes?

Vida
I wouldn't hold ur breath little hippie, but let's see?

Agave
Goodness, my baby, he'll be worried sick about me!

Five

Pentheus' *room, Palace.* **Tireseus** *enters.*

Pentheus
My mother's just been butchered, Tireseus
There is no one left for the Gods to take from me
(*In a dark place.*) It's not a good time to disturb my peace

Tireseus
Oh but it is, for your mother Agave is not deceased.

Pentheus (*sarcastic*)
Oh she's not? How, why, so all her blood is just . . .?

Tireseus
She's lost some blood, yes, but she's tough and she's survived

Pentheus
She's not dead? Then um. Okay. Where is she?

Tireseus
In the mountains

Pentheus
The mountains! She's alive in the mountains, okay, and she's there why?

Tireseus
To worship Dionysos . . .

Pentheus
BULLSHIT

Tireseus
. . . with the Bacchae

Pentheus
THEM! And that – FUCK!!!! That demonic swindling piece of foreign shit!!

Tireseus
He's your cousin

Pentheus
Are you buzzing?!
How in Zeus' name did he capture the Theban Queen from the Palace?

Tireseus
Magic

Pentheus
You lost your mind as well as your sight?!

Tireseus
Pentheus, this is your one & only opportunity to Unite

Pentheus
I'll die before uniting with that crackhead
He brainwashes women by force-feeding them mind-altering-alcoholically-infused booze!

Tireseus
This is *Good News*
Your mother *lives*
You can negotiate a lasting peace

Pentheus
I'll negotiate his torture and arrest – Zeus can attest
I don't negotiate with disorganised *ugly* drunk feminist terrorists!

Demi
Who da fuck u calling disorganised!

Vida (*finding it funny*)
Don't u start causing discord Little Miss Clipboard

Pentheus
Here's the Strategy: kill him & his Bacchae

Tireseus
You weren't always like this
When you inherited the throne you were soft and –

Pentheus
Don't *ever* call me that

Beat.

Tireseus
You were once a . . . different kind of King, sire
Before you replaced your Crown for this new militant attire
Perhaps you have become too strict?

Pentheus
I haven't been strict *enough*
I won't make that mistake again
My mother's life depends on it
Therefore the Bacchae's existence is unallowable
You do know these 'women' perform fellatio on cows n bulls?

Vida
'Fellatio'?! Says the prick who never got the *gluck gluck* from anyone!
Only 'fellatio' he could ever get is if he removed his own ribs n gave *himself* some!
Dickhead.

Pentheus
He's a Fake God, bringing shame to our family name
Like his lying mother
Zeus is not his bloody father!

Tireseus
You really believe that?

Pentheus
Did I stutter?
Okay, old man, let's say Zeus did actually fuck her
Then Semele's just another that Zeus' used n abused without a rubber
That makes Dionysos a mortal bastard baby
If you think thousands of mortal women gave birth to
Actual Gods you're an actual nutter!

Tireseus
Thousands of bastards but the Bacchae only worship one
He's invented a new Freedom & Wine
It's going Global – Liberating hearts & minds!

Pentheus
Liberating? Women are like sheep –

Tireseus
Sheep?

Pentheus
Okay not sheep but, look, *their* nature is soft okay?
They're easily influenced, it's endangering to women to liberate them
I impose Order to protect them from themselves!

Tireseus (*prophecy*)
Pentheus, Love the God in a beautiful dress, and you will cease to suffer

Pentheus
Stop shouting shite you nutter!

Tireseus
If you don't, son, Fate will rip your flesh off your skeleton
But this God can make flowers grow in the darkest parts of you, if you let him in

30 Bacchae

Pentheus
>You sound stupid
>There's no place for this foreigner here
>Thebes isn't known for being inclusive!

Tireseus
>Boy, this ain't a game of chess, this is Fate!
>The Horse took your Queen, it's already Checkmate!

Pentheus
>On my daughter's grave, Tireseus, I vow to exterminate every Bacchae. Clitus!

Tireseus *exits.*

Demi
>*Clitus?!*

Clitus (*enters*)
>Highness

Pentheus
>Draft every Theban man no matter how old or young
>Who can hold and clutch a sword.

Serene
>I'll chop the left bollock off every one of dem!

Pentheus
>Send Special Forces to the mountains and capture me a hostage!
>Then I'll rescue my mother & wipe the floor of their squad
>Let every Bacchae bitch know: I, King Pentheus am declaring war on their God!

Six

Mountains. Choral Ritual: **Bacchae** *conjure* **Dionysos** *with frenzied, wild anticipation.*

Demi
> He took the bait & declared war, let's tell Dio the plan is in motion

Niloo
> Time to awaken our God with a very special potion!

Bacchae
> We summon and conjure
> Our God to come conquer
> Compose a bloody concert
> Cos this young man won't *concur*

Bacchae *surround* **Agave**, *with chants of 'Who Are Ya' & 'Agave' intensifying the ritual.* **Niloo** *gives* **Agave** *another bottle of blood, she downs it.* **Kera** *hands her a blade. Unsure,* **Agave** *looks for guidance,* **Kera** *gestures to cut her arm,* **Agave** *does & is released into a heightened state of ecstasy, her blood spurts onto the floor, smoke gushes from it, conjuring* **Dionysos**.

Dionysos
> Woooooo!! I! LOVE! BEING! *Conjureeeed!*

Agave (*surprised*)
> It worked!

Dionysos
> Where's the orgy I'm ready I been drinking pineapple juice *all* week! What we doin who
> we shaggin who we killing?

Vida (*to* **Dionysos**)
> Ello sunshine

Dionysos
> Mummy Vida, my cousin Pentheus still don't believe in me? Even though I possessed his mother's mind n brought her to us so easily?

Vida (*aside*)
> I fear we're playing with fire with dat one, it's troubling
> Using his own mum to punish him is a hell of a fucking fing

Dionysos
> I was playing with fire when Pentheus was learning to colour in!
> Yeah I got conjured with . . . *Aunty blood!!!* . . . oh heyyy.
> Thebes, I'm back, this is a big day
> Lemme lookatchya, as I expected, Thebes is a bit bland
> Don't worry I bring the spice & heat

Bacchae
> Mmmmm

Dionysos
> I was baptised in Fire, right here in Thebes
> Semele died to save me, Hera's fire burnt her to cinders
> So I'm doomed to suffer on Earth with my sisters
> The snobbish Gods on Olympus didn't invite me to live with them
> They say being the God of Wine & Rhyme ain't worthy of an Olympian
> So fuck em: cos I am the *Wine Man*, no no I am the *Whine Man*
> From Cuba to Congo to Thailand
> Liberating hearts & minds fam
> From Scottish Highlands to Somali white sands
> I'm the sommelier rhyme-man for every nation & island!

Beat kicks in, boppy **Bacchae** *dance begins in tandem with* **Dionysos**.

Dionysos
> So thank u for the summon sisters
> Ever see a God that freestyle's stunning scriptures?

Serene
> He's good with words

Dionysos
> I'm a cunning linguist

Demi
> Even better with his tongue

Dionysos (*steps forward*)
   I invented *cunnilingus!*
   I ain't like dese friminipin-boring-ass Gods
   I'm a finger-lickin-slip-my-dick-in-n-pour-a-glass God

Bacchae
   THE ONLY GOD ON EARTH

Dionysos
   I like to wriggle with the muggles

Bacchae
   IN THE MUD & DIRT – WHAT ELSE?

Dionysos
   My daddy is Zeus

Bacchae
   BIG FLEX

Dionysos
   My mummy died to save me

Bacchae
   SHE WAS A PRINCESS

Dionysos
   Luckily Vida raised me

Bacchae
   YOUR OTHER MOTHER

Dionysos
   But Zeus didn't claim me?!

Bacchae
   SO FUCK HIS THUNDER!

Dionysos
   I'm known for travelling
   To different lands & dismantling autocratic Kings
   I'm the dazzling extravagant champion
   Can't resist liberating women from shackling
   That's dangling a carrot in front of a ravenous stallion!

Bacchae His *enemies* . . . never *see* him coming!

Dionysos
   Cos these autocrats **have cataracts**
   Bacchae gang attack like **rat-a-tat!**
   Kinky sex acts with candle wax
   Grab Agave her off her Saddleback (**and she don't get her saddle back!**)
   Squeeze grapes from Shiraz to Bacharach
   Greek Classic grammar man but we chat in slang
   I'm in my prime mate like an orangutang
   Bacchae travel from land to land **in his caravan**
   Babylon to Afghanistan women are a fan of man
   Now he's landed on Theban Palace land
   Will my Palace fam understand just cos I'm
   Half God Half Human **don't treat me like I'm Caliban!**
   Now – Women of Thebes – I'm being genuine
   Please ask urself two questions, they're imperative

Bacchae
   QUESTION 1

Dionysos
   Does ur husband wanna lick a man's arsehole?

Bacchae
   ALSO

Dionysos
   Shall I decapitate Pentheus on a mountain?

Music and dance freeze.

   What? Could be pretty lit to put the 'kill a man' in Kilimanjaro?

Bacchae
   OOOohhhh

Music and dance return.

Dionysos
   I should be careful what I say tho
   I know Theban prosecutors use rap lyrics as evidence

To sentence young immigrants & start beheading them
Treating us like refugees from war-torn countries
Who in their homelands had doctorate degrees

Yunann
Like me!

Dionysos
But now are expected to clean
Shitty piss-stained toilets cos the Western Nation
Refuses to recognise their qualifications!

Yunann
Theoretically speaking I'm more qualified than most
Western practitioners of –

Dionysos
But yo – now I've arrived it's Go Time
It's Showtime! I'm fresh off the boat like:

Bacchae
'Can I have some refuge please?'

Dionysos
Please! *How can a God be a refugee?!*

Music and dance crescendo.

Yo aunty! Shit . . . I used to fink I didn't give a fuck like a celibate
But ur the first member of my blood family I've ever met
Rah. I travelled years for this . . . I see u responded to my calling

Agave
I did and now I've . . . conjured you!

Dionysos
Not quite, I conjured you to conjure me
I light the stage & pull the strings behind the scenes

Agave
WOW wow WOW my sister's son is a real God!!! I was so wrong!

Dionysos
That's the spirit
Now lemme remind u of the rumour u created back in the day
You said that ur sister Semele:

Dionysos *clicks his fingers:* **Agave**, *as if it were years before, repeats the rumour she created.*

Agave
Spread her legs open wide as the Theban Ocean
No wonder she died during childbirth
She was infected with the sperm of a low-life rodent

Dionysos *clicks again,* **Agave** *drops out of it.*

Dionysos
But why would you lie when you knew I was Zeus? Was it jealousy?

Agave
Yes it was, regrettably
But now I've seen the error of my ways
I shall worship you as your loving Aunty

Dionysos
My mother was loving, kind and sweet
You're nothing *like* Semele

Agave
I care for you now nephew as I always have done
In ways you can't even fathom

Dionysos
Make yourself at home aunty, I'll find use for u later
But first I wanna meet my Pagan cousin Pentheus
I'm gonna mess with him, play with him, make him love me
But if he continues his blasphemous fuckry then shit will get ugly!

Demi
　He's just sent soldiers to get a Bacchae hostage too

Dionysos
　In that case I'll disguise myself as a *human* – *eww*

Serene
　As a human? *You?*

Dionysos
　Well I ain't meeting him as this sexy linguistician, uh no, not all Godly & heaven-sent
　Gotta suss him out first – I'll dress up as a Bacchae-follower
　Willingly be captured by Pentheus' regiment

Assisted by **Vida**, **Dionysos** *begins dressing in traditional Ancient Greek garb: tunic, sandals, etc.*

　I'm gonna meet Pentheus dressed as a good little immigrant
　An assimilating, 'wow Greece is such an amazing civilisation' kinda immigrant!

Serene
　U look so *different* as a mortal fam I'm cringing

Dionysos
　I pull it off no?

Serene
　U look like a beg bruv

Vida
　You look the part son, the prick'll be blissfully ignorant of the danger he's in

Dionysos
　The plan is this: I'm gonna be a Trojan Horse in Pentheus' Palace
　Dazzle him till he worships me – time to play with him!

Dionysos *exits in disguise.*

Vida
So let the Dysfunctional Family Olympic games begin!

Seven

Palace. A terrified **Clitus** *approaches a furious* **Pentheus**.

Pentheus
Get out my sight!

Clitus (*ducks behind pillar*)
Highness, our special military operation was a rip-roaring success

Pentheus
Return to my sight. Talk!

Clitus
We-we-we have captured *him*

Pentheus
Who's *him*, Clitus?!

Clitus
A *male* B-Bacchae follower

Tireseus
How *unusual*

Pentheus
A Bacchae *man*?! (*To* **Tireseus**.) Do those exist?

Tireseus
My foresight tells me this one is one of a kind

Pentheus
And I've captured him, I am the most specialest military strategist

Clitus
So special, Highness

Pentheus
I'll milk this man for every squirt of intelligence on these terrorists

Clitus
Milk this man, Highness!

Alexis (*enters*)
Majesty, he didn't resist arrest!

Tireseus
That's interesting

Pentheus
That scared to protest? They're crumbling already

Alexis
He said he doesn't fear death

Tireseus
What kind of being doesn't fear death, I wonder?

Pentheus
We'll see about that, show me this queer

Enter **Dionysos**, *disguised, 'captured' & led in by* **Alexis**.

Dionysos
Erm, so sorry I think I'm lost can someone kindly tell me why I'm here?

Pentheus
Look. At. You.

They take each other in, both captivated by seeing each other for the first time.

Dionysos
Woh

Pentheus
Don't be scared softboy
You are my first spoil of war

Dionysos
Wow
I haven't seen a *real* man before

Alexis
Choose your words wisely, you're talking to your king!

Dionysos
Which one said that?! Oh. *You.*
He tried to finger me en route to the Palace that was very uncouth of you!
But I shan't let it tarnish my otherwise wonderful experience in Thebes!

Clitus
I must say, Highness, I witnessed nothing of the sort –

Dionysos
I mean if the dextrous fingering was consensual
I would have *potentially* found it sensual
But he's got no concept of boundaries
It's discombobulating I even miss you when I'm with you is that crazy?

Alexis
Majesty, on my future babies' lives I swear I never –

Pentheus
Sh. Your babies would be better off as bastards.
(*To* **Dionysos**.) You are a very strange kind of man

Dionysos (*curtsies*)
Thank you Highness

Pentheus
Do you know what kind of man *I* am?

Dionysos
Yes! Dionysos' Mortal cousin!

Pentheus
No, you brainwashed migrant
I'm the kind of man who extinguishes cigarette butts in

my enemies' belly buttons
Now since when did the Bacchae allow men in their feminine ranks?

Dionysos
I'm the Token Testosterone, they just use me for diversity funding

Pentheus
I'm afraid I'm gonna use you too, for information
Where do your parents hail from? Ethiopian, Syrian, some type of Arabian?

Dionysos
My dad is kind of a big deal, as for my mother –

Pentheus
No one cares about your mother.
Have you seen *my* mother, the Queen?

Dionysos
She's with the girls doing girly things I feel *masculine* in ur presence bro's it's *delicious*

Pentheus
Do you like doing girly things too?

Dionysos
Love it

Pentheus
Dionysos gets involved in all that fruity stuff, does he?

Dionysos
The way his hips gyrate to the rhythm –

Pentheus
Sh. What are this Girlyman's demands?

Dionysos
Not very demanding tbh he's just like drink wine sex it up & 'no oppression please!'

Pentheus
Now listen properly, peasant, I wasn't asking about his *personality*
He's taken my mother hostage, so what are his military demands from *me*?

Dionysos
Bacchic rule in Thebes

Pentheus
Deluded, Bacchic rule, indeed!
He knows he'll never be welcome in Thebes, why's he come?

Tireseus
Fate would have it

Pentheus
Shut it

Dionysos
You should totally meet him he's the best

Pentheus
Has he, like, you know, sort of, ever, mentioned me to you?

Dionysos
For citizenship and an authentic Souvlaki
I will reveal all

Pentheus
Don't get cute
Last chance before I feed you to The Bull in the pits
I like watching him mince men, it gives me pleasure
The Bull is my big bulky Bacchae shredder.

Dionysos
Far be it from me to kink-shame you

Pentheus
What in Zeus' name are you?

Dionysos
Great guess, hole in one, Nepo-baby that's me! And you need me!

Pentheus
Aye, like I need dysentery

Dionysos
Ew u got dysentery? You got it from *him* didn't you? The guard with the intrepid finger.

Pentheus
Kill him!

Alexis
Thank you!

Dionysos
Kill your bargaining tool with Dionysos?

Pentheus
I'm not bargaining with him!
His mum got killed for being a slut
Then his aunty didn't want him & gave him up for adoption
Now he's here come to take his *Mummy Issues* out on us!

Tireseus
Pentheus, don't be blinded by your ignorance

Pentheus
Stop peppering my interrogation with your interjections, it's so annoying!
Take him to The Bull!

Dionysos
If you lock me up you won't survive the night so I wish you lots of luck!

Pentheus
Save your nursery rhymes for prison!

Dionysos
>My God will free me
>Easy fucking peasy!

Guards take **Dionysos,** *all leaving only* **Tireseus** *&* **Pentheus**, *his expression changed.*

Pentheus
>What in the Hades . . .
>A Bacchae asylum seeker threatening the King of Thebes . . . what the f –

Eight

The Pits. Lighting is a confined circle. **Bull** *batters* **Dionysos** *till he's exhausted.*

Bull
>Why you not bleeding
>I smashed you

Dionysos
>I don't bleed
>Cos I'm *free*

Bull
>Free

Dionysos
>You see?
>–

Bull
>No
>Smash time again
>Need blood

Dionysos
>Got none I'm a God

Bull
>God?

Dionysos
Yeah God

Bull
Of what?

Dionysos
Wine
And a good time

Bull
And
–
Rhyme?

Dionysos (*caught off guard*)
Yeah Rhyme God too!
Divine raps it's true!

Bull
Boo!

Dionysos
Ha yeah! It's cool init?
But them Gods up on Olympus won't make a space for me
Apollo gets a space u know – the God of Poetry –
whatever!
How's dis for poetry, Apollo: My Dick's Bigger & I Rhyme Better!

Bull
Ha
Yeah . . .
–
Still have to smash you

Dionysos
Wait wait – What u in here for? Heard ur a child-killer?

Bull
Not true
Fake News.

Dionysos
Who u kill then?

Bull
Pentheus' daughter

Serene
Da fuck?!

Demi
Why would he kill her??

Dionysos
Dat was *you*?

Bull
My job: Protect Princess
But I kill
Mistake
Now he hate
Me

Dionysos
Beautifully chunky man, before that incident, who did u *used* to be?

Bull
Greatest most fantastic Warrior in all of Thebes

Dionysos
Okayyyy BigMan I'd sayyy you used to cause a bit of trouble

Bull
Smash one hundred guys
Don't even pull a muscle

Dionysos
Paint me a picture with words rudeboi we're vibing now
I'm feeling this dynamic duo – u feel it too?

Bull (*intense emotion*)
I feel
I very
Feel

Dionysos
There's a fine line between cumming & crying n he's straddling dat fence to completion

Bull
Few years ago Theban Women hear rumours about Bacchae
They like sound of it
Pentheus' daughter like it too
But Pentheus say Bacchae bad
She want to play Bacchae
So she be sad

Demi
Just a young girl tryna thrive

Bull
Then one day
Pentheus' daughter dress up
With her little friends
From Palace
To Forest
Drunk with wine
Pretending to be Bacchae
She creep behind big massive bull
Stab its eye
The bull scream so loud
It reach Palace
Pentheus hear it
He think: *Oh no, maybe real Bacchae actually arrive*
He tell me: strike them like Zeus' lightning
He tell me: Bacchae hoes too cantankerous for my liking

Serene
He actually call us cantankerous hoes?

Vida
Weirdo using words he don't even know

Serene
Init! You'd never do that Vida, you're too magnanimous

Bull
>I find
>I break . . . I kill
>But they *cry*
>These little girls
>Not real Bacchae
>Mistake
>I carry Princess' little body to Palace
>After I slaughter
>Pentheus' heart turn fire
>Recognise her
>*His own daughter*

Nava
>Poor Pentheus

Dionysos
>Bro it wasn't ur fault, u followed an order – plz tell me u defended urself?

Bull
>I say I enormous sorry King

Dionysos
>Incredibly articulate apology

Bull
>But it just one of those things

Dionysos
>Wow

Bull
>But now he not soft friendly King no more
>He say I must pay
>He build me prison
>I can never run
>And he name me *Bull*
>To forever remember
>What I done

Dionysos
You're a scapegoat

Bull
No
I a Bull

Dionysos
You kill for Pentheus & he locks u up
Is that Law & Order or some villain shit? I'd say he's a . . .?

Bull
. . . *hypocrite*

Dionysos
Time for . . .

Bull
. . . revenge

Dionysos
Yes. Wanna know a secret?

Bull
No

Dionysos
No?

Bull
No
Yes

Dionysos
Yes?

Bull
Yes
No
Yes – final answer

Dionysos
I'm gonna free you – don't panic

Dionysos *summons the stage lights above to move, lighting state goes from a confined circle to broader diameter, therefore 'freeing' the* **Bull**.

Bull
Cheeky Small Man that's magic!

Dionysos
Yep, now listen Mr Catfish, let's give u a *new* name.

Bull
Bull

Dionysos
Yep – and you wanna change your name from Bull to . . .?

Bull
Bull

Dionysos
Oh. No. Hear this: You Are Not An Animal
So what *new* name would you like?

Bull
Bull

Dionysos
But bro

Bull
Without the 'the'. No
The Bull
Just
. . . Bull
It feels . . . cool

Dionysos
Cool?

Bull
Like it could be short for . . . Bullanor!

Dionysos
Really?!

Bull

Or maybe something to do with my muscles or my battle scars?
Or Kabull!! Yeah, cos my great-grandma's from Afghanistan!

Dionysos

Why don't you try something a little more subtle?

Bull

Why you wanna burst my bubble?!
BUBULL!

Dionysos

Fantastic! God damn!

Bubull

Yes. Now Bubull is free thanks to you, Funny Little God Man.
But I have one request

Dionysos

Be my guest

Bubull

I want to walk through the palace one last time with my head held high

Dionysos

Say no more
I'll make you invisi-bull so the guards won't see you as you walk through the door

Bubull

I hate guard Alexis
He call me Big Bull Little Balls

Dionysos

I'll deal with him while u enjoy freedom – how's that hey?

Bubull

That. Is exactly what I hoped you'd say.

Bull *glides into the horizon in amazement,* **Dionysos** *leaves cell, now face-to-face with a confused* **Alexis.**

Alexis
　　How did you get out?! Hey I can't let you through!

Dionysos
　　You've not learnt to host hospitably have u?

Dionysos *steps towards him.*

　　I'm gonna need you to twerk for me
　　Shake it to show you're sorry b
　　Shake as an apology

Alexis
　　I don't want to have to use my weapon!

Dionysos
　　Face down arse-up rubeboi, jiggle it

Alexis
　　You're just a follower of that Son Of A Whore you freak immigrant!

Dionysos *summons a stage light to spotlight* **Alexis**, *he's blinded by it.*

Alexis
　　Wait! Please I got a babies on the way wait –

Dionysos
　　Don't fight it, only fools fight Fate

Blackout. The sound of struggle & death.

Nine

Lights up. **Bacchae** *break the action.*

Demi
　　HOLD UP TIME OUT! Fuck this!

Serene
Time out? Demi we don't do intervals we discussed dis!

Demi
Dio, if we indiscriminately kill innocent guards then we're da same as our enemies!

Yunann
My darling, let me check your temperature, got a fever or the flu?
Are you done questioning the son of Zeus or you wanna continue?

Dionysos
Demi the Guard was complicit
It don't make us even slightly hypocritic

Demi
Since when is this what we do?

Yunann (*to* **Dionysos**)
Demi's always been holier-than-thou but no mortal can be holier-than-*you!*

Demi
Shut up you shitty little dentist

Yunann
I'm not a dentist!

Demi
Don't question my idolatry
The DDC policy states we overthrow monarchies
But we don't become *like* these dickheads u dickhead n start killing wantonly!

Everyone in stunned silence like: oh shit **Demi** *just called their God a dickhead.*

Dionysos
Demi . . . u know what . . . I hear u. Yunann, it's no big issue. All good.

Serene (*beat*)
> Awkward . . .

Demi
> Stop stirring! I'm Head of Strategy young lady, big people address stuff

Serene
> Na u know u effed up! U called Dio a dickhead ur dead now Demi!!

Demi
> You're silly and I don't have time for you

Serene
> Hades is gonna make the Underworld so nice for you
> Smear your clipboard with blood, piss n poo

Demi
> Why does everyone come for my fucking clipboard!! You'd be lost without it!

Serene
> Serving u hellish bland Western food, beige on beige, yuck, no seasoning, nuffin!

Agave
> I am starving

Niloo
> Wolf liver for a gut reset, Majesty?

Agave *takes it, starts gnawing away passionately.*

Dionysos
> The guard called me a Son of a Whore, he deserved it!

Kera
> He was born a man, therefore he deserved it

Beat.

Vida
> You're a God sunshine u can't let mum-cusses affect u!

Dionysos
I come home n even that pumplex Pentheus reminding me I don't belong!

Vida
Ah your cousin hit you where it hurts yeah

Dionysos
I blame the other Gods for not legitimising me!
Like how is God of Wine not good enough to be on Olympus?
I'm better than skatty little Hermes what the flip does he do?

Serene
Dat yout is redundant we got Amazon Prime & Deliveroo bruv we do not need you!

Agave (*privately*)
Let's make this chewing business easier.

Demi
Dio, the plan was to be a Trojan Horse

Agave (*sound of metal on bone, sharpening teeth*)
I could devour a horse!

Demi
Gods don't beg mortals to believe in them, it makes u look weak bro

Serene
Dio she said you're *weak* u gonna have dat?

Demi
So teach him a lesson he'll never forget, den he'll have no choice but to believe in you!

Dionysos
You're right, okay lemme think, Theban women love us right?
Even Pentheus' daughter wanted to be like us proper

Agave
> My beautiful granddaughter, I sharpen these canines in your honour!

Serene
> She's bit pyscho init?

Dionysos
> I'm gonna invite every single Theban woman to join us in the mountains!!!

Dionysos *creates a melodious a capella sound with his vocals, his exact Pied Piper beat from the opening is brought to life in the sound design.*

Dionysos
> The Pied Piper has just touched down in town
> Every Theban Woman'll join us by following my sound

Serene
> I love it when u do Houdini shit

Nava
> A million new women, the orgies are gonna get . . . overwhelming

Serene
> Seducing the women of Thebes with a beat is mythical!

Dionysos
> Pentheus will certainly worship me after I execute my greatest trick of all!

Demi
> I love getting Dictators back with innovative strategies, it's so refreshing not to kill em all?

Serene
> Such a nerd, so dorky

Dionysos
> Pentheus, you're about to witness a God in all his Glory!

Sound of beat gets louder, infectious and trickles into next scene.

Ten

Bubull *walks through the Palace as a free man, invisible to all except for –*

Tireseus
Hello

Bubull
Of *all* people it is the blind man who can see me?
That is enormously ironic

Tireseus
Freedom suits you well . . . Bubull

Bubull
Thank you old friend, LittleGodMan has freed me
I so excited to revenge on Pentheus

Tireseus
Bubull, if you choose Revenge you can never be Free

Pentheus (*from offstage*)
Leon, after the day I've had, you better be hearing good news!

Bubull
Pentheus
Don't tell him you saw me

Tireseus
Even if I did . . . who would believe me?

Bubull
Genius!

Bubull *exits,* **Tireseus** *lurks in the shadows,* **Leon the Messenger** *and* **Pentheus** *enter.*

Leon
Humblest Sincerest
Apologies Most Gracious Majesty for what I am about to say:
But bro, our women are leaving Thebes in *biblical floods*

towards the mountains
It's like they're spellbound following some magic

Pentheus
He's brainwashed more?! Get them all back at once Leon

Leon
Highness, I'm not sure we have sufficient infantry to retrieve them all

Pentheus
My own army have turned into sissies have they? And you. *Biblical floods* indeed, since when did a little runt like you have such a flair for the dramatic?

Leon
Highness, I admit I've been taking in the classics as of late and I'm easily influen –

Pentheus
Learn to identify a rhetorical question!

Leon
Yes of course I will –

Pentheus
Don't waste precious time formulating a sentence – go bloody get them!
What part of at-bloody-once on-bloody-sight evades your comprehension?!

Leon
At once sir

Leon *exits.*

Pentheus (*to himself*)
Zeus have mercy, why would they all leave?

Tireseus (*reappearing*)
I can answer that question
I myself spoke with one of the *many* women who have left to join the Bacchae . . .

Pentheus
> . . . yes?

Tireseus
> I asked her *why*
> She said because when Thebes competes in the sport of Epikyrios
> Her husband gets mad when his team loses

Pentheus
> And?

Tireseus
> And he beats her out of anger

Pentheus
> He's a proud Theban, proud to a fault maybe, but proud nonetheless

Tireseus
> So then I asked her what happens if Thebes *wins* the match?

Tireseus *pauses, finding it difficult to say.*

Pentheus
> What's wrong with all the men today? *Speak,* Tireseus, no need for a dramatic . . . pause

Tireseus
> She said he beats her out of joy

Tireseus *exits, beat.*

Pentheus
> Leon!

Leon *returns, half-dressed in armour.*

> Why've you not left yet?
> Go up the mountains & deliver him a message, a promise:
> Return my women or my archers will shoot a thousand flaming arrows at the forest

Leon

The terrain will spread a tornado of wildfire, scorching indiscriminately without prejudice . . .

Beat.

Pentheus

Exactly. An exceptional strategic manoeuvre from me! He'll have to release the women cos he's desperate to appear like a good little feminist!
Now go tell the terrorist!
But be careful don't do anything stupid, Leon, you're the only trustworthy man I have left in this

Eleven

Mountains. **Agave**, *munching a wolf drumstick, proudly overlooking the audience*

Sound of **Dionysos**' *Pied Piper instrumental pulsating in the background.*

Demi

Rah! Bare of them there's like a gazillion!

Niloo

Dio evacuated the entire female population with an instrumental das mental!

Serene

How greeeeedy!

Demi

And if I do say so myself, I really spruced up the manifesto too

Nava

Omg twinning I also manifested new recruits!

Serene

Dat ain't what a manifesto is bruv

Agave
 I, Agave, Bacchae Queen, welcome you, Women of
 Thebes, to Freedom's Dominion!
 Unshackle your femininity! Together we can conquer
 anything!

Vida
 Fill up your cups! Slurp it all up! Time for Girly Drinks!

Vida *leads the* **Bacchae***'s choral ritual: commemorating their newfound strength in numbers.*

 WHO ARE YA WHO ARE YA?!

Bacchae
 We are the Bacchae
 Bacchae Bacchae Bacchae!

Vida
 We vow to

Bacchae
 Euthanise Neutralise Parasites!

Vida
 If we have to die fighting, it'll be a

Bacchae
 Glorified Gratified Sacrifice!

Vida
 Wine in the cup! Drink it all up!

Bacchae
 Glug! Flood our livers! Glug!
 Flood their rivers! With blood!

Vida
 We offer

Bacchae
 Immolation Libation Oblation

Kera (*to* **Agave**)
Look a messenger!

Agave
A gift for me?!

Bacchae
In the name of Dionysos!

Leon (*enters*)
I have a message from his Royal Eminence King Pentheus
For Dionysos: Militia Leader of the Bacchae, Recognised
as a Terrorist Organisation under
Ladies
Listen Ladies Please –

As **Leon** *is delivering his speech* **Agave** *runs and chases him offstage.*

Vida
Where u going come back you skatty Queen!

Serene
Shit she's pounced him!

All
Ooohhh

Nava
Oh Hades she's stripping him

Demi
May Aphrodite protect him

Niloo
Look at his little thing it's so cold it's shrivelling

Yunann
They shrivel out of fear, the brain sends messages to the
Penile Suspensory Ligament

Leon (*offstage*)
OUAAAAAHHH!!!

All
AHHHHH!!!!!!

Demi
She didn't just do dat

Vida
She did it, she's a doer

Nava
I knew something like this was gonna happen today

Sunny
How?

Nava
Mercury's in retrograde

Having devoured **Leon**, **Agave** *gleefully returns onstage to the group.*

Demi
You ate the messenger!
Never eat the messenger

Agave *spits a few of her own teeth out.*

Agave
He was delicious!

Serene
Babe u got a toe in ur tooth

Agave
I sharpened my fangs yet the toe knuckle is still surprisingly hard to chew!

Yunann
That is partly due to larger metatarsals, stubbier phalanges & tissues

Vida (*to* **Agave**)
Ur too damn trigger happy, don't make me have to tranquilise you!

Kera
Leave her be she's exemplary

Vida (*to* **Kera**)
What kinda nasty-ass show she fink we're performing?

Kera
Never thought I'd see the day Badgal Vida became an advocate for Trigger Warnings

Beat.

Vida
See these fists? They're Gender Neutral. They'll kill a prick for being a predaTOR
OR kill a bitch premature 'fore she gets to hit menopause!

Kera
If ur not willing to kill *any* man to be free
Then the word Freedom is an imposter in ur vocabulary

Vida
Okay bitch. Lemme break it down for clarity: Bacchic Laws exist to protect our family
I won't let ur young dumb rebellious vanity to turn our Greek Victory into a Greek Tragedy
And you lot, no need to clap for me
For lyrically battering this intellectually challenged-fiend, who developed big ideas n
fundamentalist fantasies after popping too many acid tabs laced with crack at *Glastonbury*
(Suck on dat u illiterate little shit n think twice next time u challenge me . . .& my *vocabulary!*)

Kera
Okay, I'm illiterate. Sometimes words aren't needed

Kera *pulls out her blade, looks at* **Vida** *like a young lion vying for supremacy.*

My knife is a woman of few words
Short attention-spanned & brainless

But when she does speak:
slash slash slash
She's *onomatopoeic*

Vida *disarms* **Kera**.

Demi
Vida, I disagree with this fanatic too, she not blessed with morals or a dress sense
But we don't attack our own, ignore her, u ain't gotta be best friends

Vida (*returns the knife to* **Kera**)
Demi just saved your life child

Agave (*beat*)
Vida . . . don't be a pussy!

Demi
Zeus, have patience!!!

Agave
You're the one with the reputation for cutting your husbands face off you Crazy Bitch
I'm just trying to be like you! No one would fuck with Vida not even Zeus!

Vida
Demi take her before I –

Agave *pulls away from* **Demi** *and stands by* **Kera**.

Agave
Now look I don't want to be the cause of a Bacchae divide
But Vida, I know you have such a soft side alongside your tough side
Aww you could have left baby Dionysos to die
But you chose to raise a youth in Asia
Instead of voluntary euthanasia!
Who's your mummy . . . Vida! Who's your daddy . . . Vida!

Demi
Nope, absolutely not today, bitch

Vida

You know what: Yeah I was Dio's mummy and his daddy, I had to be
What u fink I can say no Zeus I'd rather not do it?! He'd say:
Blud Are You Stupid?! When I Come For You With Dis Arrow Don't Fink Dat I'm Cupid!
So no – It's not my soft side kicking in, that woman died years ago
And when I asked Zeus why he'd come to *me*, in *Asia*, with this Theban orphan baby
Rather than his living breathing Aunty Agave you know what he say?
I *did* take the baby boy to her, but she turned him away!

Agave

You know nothing about my conversation with Zeus that day
I do not answer to plebs!

Vida

Yo, Yunann, you used to be a doctor right?

Yunann

No.
I have a doctorate in witchcraft

Vida

Even better. How can we fix her?
Cos if we don't I will kill her

Yunann

My prognosis would ordinarily be hypnosis
But her accelerated condition (particularly pertaining to leaving the messenger toeless)
Renders neurological intervention rather hopeless

Vida

In layman's terms . . .?

Yunann
Oh she's fucked mate.

Vida
Can't Dio just un-possess her tho?

Yunann
No. She's too far gone

Dionysos *suddenly appears, in an incredibly playful mood.*

Dionysos
Yooo! I feel so cheeky!
How's Pentheus gonna say I'm not a God now?
Houdini made 1 elephant disappear, I just did 1 million gyal!

Vida
Dio, listen son –

Dionysos (*silly mood*)
You raised a *badman* u know dat mum?!
Now how can Pentheus possibly not admit I'm Zeus' son!

Demi
Let's get outta of Thebes our work here is done, Pentheus lost, The Bacchae have won!

Vida
No! Not with her and her merry band of radical fanaticals
Agave's gonna fracture us, leave her behind with these New Gen Bacchanals

Dionysos
Yo what happened, what did I miss?

Serene
Agave ate the messenger alive like he was breakfast

Yunann
Anatomically speaking she consumed an unproductive portion of his reproductive organ, as for his carcass, she dined on it till he was heartless

Serene
Literally

Dionysos
Shit I missed dat I got distracted celebrating with a few sexy . . . (*mumbles, trailing off*)

Kera
Dio we think Agave's a perfect addition
Her militant worship aligns with your vision

Demi
Not all of us – let the record state!

Kera
She's got the traction with the Theban women
Without her they won't be so willing

Mertha
I had writers' block but she weirdly reinspired my erotic fiction

Sunny
And she kindly donated one molar n two canines to the cause

Dionysos
I am hearing both sides of the argument – *I get it!*
For now . . . (*to* **Yunann**) we can just sedate her a bit, right medic?

Vida
I asked her already forget it
Dis demented eccentric would be an insomniac under anaesthetic

Dionysos (*still in silly mood*)
Let me chat to her, no wozza, I'll dumb it down for her in phonetics
(*As if she's hard of hearing.*) *ELL OH YU*
Aunty Agave you're really feeling free hey?

Agave
You bloody well know I am, now bring me another mammal to gobble without de-lay!

Dionysos
Shame u killed the messenger
He was just a boy, coulda been your son

Agave
In Thebes we use bastards like you as messengers, so if they die, no matter

Dionysos
I'm a fucking God!

Agave
There's that temper! It's very proletarian
God or not you *were* raised by a barbarian

Dionysos
SHUT UP! Don't ever compare yourself to Vida or Semele!

Agave *flinches in the way that anyone would when a God shouts at you.*

Vida
Dio just leave it, it's fine son

Agave
I want MY son!

Dionysos
Can't you see what this has done to me?!
I lost my mum, Zeus didn't wanna know, why didn't any of you want me?

Agave *takes a deep, sincere breath, moved by* **Dionysos'** *outburst.*

Agave
Oh Goodness me, *son*, you think I don't see your pain?
Oh you're so hurt
(*With a mother's warmth.*) Oh come here

Beat, she edges towards him.

Don't you want a hug from mummy?

Beat.

Come here sunshine

Beat.

Can you forgive me for leaving you?

Dionysos *inches towards her.*

You know I didn't have a choice

Dionysos *nods as he tears up.*

Power turned you into a monster, didn't it?

Dionysos *is on the cusp of bursting with emotion now.*

But it's okay . . . I'm still your mum & you're still my son

They hug.

My Pentheus.

Dionysos
No! NO! I'm Dio – I'm not him!!

Agave
Where's my boy, my Pen Pen?
You're not him! Can't fool me! Nice try, trickster!

Dionysos (*composing*)
You're right, Aunty, I am not him

Demi
Don't take it personal, she's outta her mind

Dionysos
You lot stay put and don't let her out of your sight
Let her eat whatever or whoever she likes

Agave
I'm ravenously hungry!

Dionysos
Let her be completely free

Kera
Yes God, leave it with me

Agave
What will my next prey be I wonder?

Dionysos
I think it'll be a hell of a catch
Aunty, you're such a great hunter

Agave
I am! NIMROD! TRAPPER! SHIKARI!

Vida (*knows he's up to something sinister*)
Dio . . .?

Serene
Can't we just leave please, Thebes gives me the creeps man

Demi
Dio let's leave, have a big orgy, few drinks, then see what's next on the DDC?
There's this Pharaoh misbehaving in Egypt
Or if we don't mind the cold, in Russia there's this eejiat –

Vida (*to* **Dio**)
I *know* you boy, don't let your temper blind you

Dionysos
I'm going back in – and leave the scene to me, don't intervene

Kera
Hell yeah: Kill First, Leave After

Demi
Back in for *what*?

Dionysos
My Pentheus

Twelve

Back in the Palace.

Pentheus
   Tireseus – where the hell is Leon the Messenger?

Tireseus
   Sadly, Leon is dead

Pentheus
   Shit *no*! I specifically ordered him not to die!

Tireseus
   And your army got spooked by the female exodus & fled

Pentheus
   I am surrounded by cowards!

Tireseus
   You're not surrounded by anyone, you are all alone

Pentheus
   I don't need anyone! I fear no Mortal!

Tireseus
   You are no match for a God –

Pentheus
   Get. Lost! I'm sick of your shite advice! Go! Leave. Now!!

Tireseus (*walking away*)
   The wilderness can be bloody heartless
   Even your shadow abandons you when you're in total darkness!

Blackout.

Thirteen

Lights up. **Dionysos** *has appeared behind* **Pentheus**. **Tireseus** *is on the margins with* **Vida**.

Dionysos
Boo. Hello you

Pentheus
How in the Hades did you break free?!

Dionysos
Dionysos freed me n sent me back to negotiate with you

Pentheus
He killed my absolute favourite messenger!
I should kill you and return the favour!

Dionysos
Agave ate him

Pentheus
She . . . what . . . ate, as in . . .?

Dionysos
Eaten yes
And bro, it was messy at best
When posh people get too hungry it always ends in an eaten mess.
Now, your mother (and excuse me for saying this I know it's not bro-code to cuss mums
and you know me bro, I'm far from a misogynist, *I got women friends!!*)
But she makes me sick
That one there is one *crazy* bitch
Respectfully.

Pentheus
Dionysos is making her crazy! Brainwashing her! This isn't *her*

Dionysos
She came to us begging to join, but she doesn't fit in
(*Emotions betraying him.*) She's too toxic, cruel, heartless –

Pentheus (*pouncing on vulnerability he's detecting*)
Let me help you
You wanna give her back I can take her off your hands?

Dionysos
... Okay ... (*Formulating plan.*) That would work perfectly
...
I can bring the Bacchae here and we can negotiate?

Pentheus
What kind of gullible fool do you think I am?

Dionysos
How about ... I take you to see the Bacchae in the mountains?

Pentheus
No! I just want my mother –

Dionysos
See them singing slithering writhing wriggling

Pentheus
I – I don't, look, well, I mean, if that's what it takes to save my mother
Fuck it I'm a man
I'll face it face-to-face
Man to man
Like a man

Dionysos
I'm the only man they've ever seen and not killed

Pentheus
So ... we need to disguise me?

Dionysos
Precisely – hmm, you'll have to look *really unthreatening*, u can't just put a big coat on

Pentheus
No ... I'd have to *put women's clothes on*

Dionysos *conjures the wardrobe.*

Dionysos You got such great ideas man

Pentheus
Thank you. Wait – no! Obviously I couldn't
Go round dressing like a woman
That's wrong that's . . .

Dionysos
What?

Pentheus
Make me look . . . I'd be . . .

Dionysos Go on . . .

Pentheus
I'd seem . . . *soft*

Light on **Vida** *&* **Tireseus** *lurking in shadows.*

Vida (*to* **Tireseus**)
I want to change Fate, is it too late to try it?

Tireseus
We always have Choice before our Fate is decided

Vida *goes towards the wardrobe & disappears behind it.*

Dionysos
Soft? Scared to feel soft?
U think it's less scary to be hard, cover yourself with armour n steel?
I'd find it much scarier *not* to feel.
An who says who can wear what? So silly, wear anything, be flippin free!
'Gender', 'identity', 'sexuality – what frivolous ridiculous mortal concoctions
'Ooh I can't wear that, Oooh I can't sex them, that would make me x, y or zee'
Blud. Gods would never be troubled by such a thing
So why the fuck would it trouble a fucking KING!

So, if you *do* 'dress as a woman'
To face the fearsome Bacchae & rescue your own mother
That would be so *soft* blud n guess *what* blud – *soft's* bloody *gangsta*!

Pentheus
You're an idiot, mostly, but you do make a wise argument

Dionysos
Cannot take any credit bro
Dionysos taught me everything I know

Pentheus
So, look I –
If we're gonna do it
Gotta make sure I look
Nice – Look right
Right
Look right.
Right?

Dionysos
Right

Pentheus
Right
Yeah

Dionysos
Yeah,
 exactly, now have we, got something specific in mind?

Pentheus
I've not dressed up as a woman for a *long* time
Since I was a child
That was my mum's clothes & now really and truly
I don't really think they . . . those dresses would suit me

Dionysos
Agave's dresses?

Pentheus
Yes it's
Nice and that
But I'm older, more muscular now
So it'll probably be a bit tight round my back
Same with the tights round my thighs
If I try and it snaps she'll go mad . . . when she gets back

Dionysos (*empathising*)
You really miss her don't you?

Pentheus
Well . . . (*giving in*) course I do

Dionysos Even tho she's been engaging in Bacchanalia?

Pentheus (*softening*)
Still my mum . . . I'm . . . still her son . . .

Beat, as they share an identical pain.

You said you'd play dress up as a kid?
Who would you play dress up with?

Pentheus
With . . . me. There was no one to . . . I couldn't just *play* per se, I was raised to be King!

Dionysos
Shame u, didn't have a, I dunno, *cousin*, or someone to play dress up with . . .

Pause, loaded.

Pentheus
What? (*Beat, has he clocked?*) Like raiding mum's wardrobe, wearing all her shit?!

Dionysos
Yeah!

Pentheus
And she's like that's enough kids!

Dionysos

Running out the Palace grounds to play and she's like *you two cousins* come right back!

Pentheus

Like dressing up as our mums and like doing impressions of them and shit like that!
And like . . . like having sleepovers and like *giggling* to the bedtime stories

Dionysos

Cuddling non-stop!

Pentheus

Yeah . . . (*Breaking tone.*) So we doing this drag shit or what?
Getting me into weird conversations – you sure like to drag shit out a lot

Dionysos

Shall we go sneak into her room together and see?

Pentheus

I'll erm pick something out, just, leave it with me

Beat, **Pentheus** *can't help but smile. Relieved, exits.*

Dionysos (*to audience*)

I know u see me getting all pally over there
I'm just getting him comfortable – I put the pally in palliative care.

Fourteen

Agave's *bedroom, Palace.*

Agave's *wardrobe.* **Pentheus** *takes off his clothing, as he opens the doors the light shines on him, illuminating, almost God-like. He selects a dress, tights, shoes, and dresses himself. Only at the end does he finally look directly at the light, the mirror, to admire his reflection. Inhaling, he starts to gently sob, for his mother, his* *daughter and for a freedom that he longs for. Exhaling, he goes to shut the door when a figure emerges from it, his voice a mix of hope & fear.*

Pentheus
Mum?

Vida
Not quite, son
I come from Agave.

Pentheus
If you're lying you'll learn the hard way –

Vida
Talk like that –

Pentheus
My guards will rip your –

Vida
Your nearest guard is 20 seconds away.
By the time he arrives you'll be circumcised.

Pentheus *looks down between his legs at the dress.*

Pentheus
Did Dionysos send you?

Vida
I'm a God-send, you could say that
And I forgive you for this big talk.
Boy I know what it's like to have to be tough, terrifying
Just to feel safe
I know the second I relax and be *soft* –

Pentheus
You're dead

Vida
I get it, the King gotta be a lion just so you can be the lamb
u truly are.
You can trust me, son

Pentheus
Why should I?

Vida
Cos it takes one to know one.
But if I can give you some motherly advice
Don't be a lion for your cousin tonight
And everything, everything, will be alright.

Pentheus
So is my mother not completely brainwashed?

Vida
Not the mother part of her
That part can't be lost

Pentheus
We can still cure my mum?

Vida
I think you're the cure, she just needs her son

Beat, a shared understanding.

Pentheus
You're their leader, aren't you?

Vida (*laughs it off*)
Why do u say that, hun?

Pentheus
Dunno, guess it takes one to know one

Dionysos *appears at* **Pentheus'** *side of the door.*

Dionysos
Yo! Who u talking to, ur imaginary friend?

Vida *hides,* **Dionysos** *doesn't realise she's there.*

Dionysos (*moved*)
Damn . . .

Beat.

Pentheus
   Here I am
   How do I look, be honest, no banter

Dionysos
   You look . . . like a beautiful gangsta

Dionysos *takes in the new* **Pentheus**, **Vida** *exits unseen by* **Dionysos**.

Fifteen

Mountains. **Bubull** *is, very drunkenly, singing his heart out.*

Bubull (*sings the chorus of 'You Raise Me Up', and the following to the same tune*)

   From the Pits to the Mountains
   Zero to Hero and counting!!
   This wine is enormously outstanding!

Serene
   You like wine yeah Bubull?

Bubull
   I'm gonna give all the sexy ladies a special cuddle
   I feel so nice so special

Demi
   He might start to show *us* how special he feels in a moment
   if we ain't careful

Bubull
   For real I love you guys
   I know I have the vine in me
   But you guys raise me
   UP!

Demi
   Yup! Bubull has risen!

Kera
And very soon your revenge will be given

Vida *enters, her energy different.*

Demi
Where you been?

Vida
Scouting the landscape

Demi
Since when did you become a forager?

Vida
Who are *you* fam, my Probation Officer?

Nava (*to* **Bull**)
I just love you! So glad Dio freed you, it was the best surprise

Bubull
I have never met anyone so happy, why are you so nice?

Nava
I escaped a stoning that my brother organised, since that I learned to appreciate the fuck outta life

Serene
Look, Dionysos and . . . who is dat?

Vida
Pentheus

Demi
Is it?

Serene
Moving like bezzie friends

Serene *points to* **Dionysos** *&* **Pentheus** *climbing the mountain in the distance.*

Kera
Time for revenge

Bubull
Why are they so bright? He's shimmering
(*Shouts.*) You're shining, Dionysos, you really are! And
Pentheus . . .
(*Retching.*) . . . I don't want . . .

Serene
Too much wine for your first time?

Bubull
I need be free

Nava
You're free here with us, Uncle Bubull

Bubull
Revenge not good for me

Kera
You can help us blend Pentheus into custard & watch him
crumble, Bubull

Bubull
Maybe Kera you not free
I love you but have to leave you
To be free . . . adieu, small creatures

Bubull *runs off into the horizon, truly free.*

Serene
Shit he really dipped! Kera u freaked him out ur too emo
man too crazy!

Kera
He's just another weak-minded man don't blame me

Nava
He's too pure for this earth

Kera
He's too soft

Vida
Maybe soft is good

Kera (*overhearing*)
  Soft will get u killed

Agave
  Soft will get you gutted in ur sleep

Kera *rewards* **Agave** *with a bite of wolf meat as if she's been a good dog.*

Serene
  You two are on some creepy codependent shit

Agave (*chewing*)
  Wolf meat will no longer suffice for me I'm a lion hunter
  I'll watch it vomit when I kill it then I'll lick it!
  My favourite meal: Sick & Blood

Cringey appropriating gestures, impersonating **Vida**.

  'Sick blud!' Hahahaha!

Kera
  Don't worry, we'll find you a lion

Serene
  U need to be sectioned bruv

Vida
  This is too fucking far – this ain't right
  Change of plan – we won't be sacrificing Pentheus tonight

Yunann
  What?

Serene
  Swear?

Vida
  We hang back, let Dio make the call

Mertha
  But we've got Pentheus in our cauldron

Kera
  Dio's brought him to us, so we're gonna maul him

Vida
He can deal with it alone, he doesn't need you

Kera
Sorry Vida, but no one made u our leader

All bar **Serene**, **Demi** *&* **Nava** *gather round* **Kera**, **Yunann** *is undecided.*

Kera
Looks like you're overruled, sister

Vida
You think *I'll* follow *you?*

Kera
Course I don't, embrace retirement, old lady, you've earned it

Demi
Nah man, what's with this internal rebellion?

Yunann
Neurolingustically speaking, during times of turmoil
The brain finds it excruciatingly hard to stay loyal
But Loyalty is essential for unity and –

Kera (*to* **Yunann**)
Stop talking stupid n go chew a toothpick!

Yunann
I don't *have* any cos I'm still not a dentist

Kera (*to* **Demi**)
It's a takeover, babe. We don't wanna be nomads no more!
Who wants to keep travelling *nation to nation?* No one!
We need a Home not a DDC, we're done
But we ain't won till the King's – hung
In our God's motherland

Vida
Dio's got a heart, he ain't gonna let u do shit – *I raised a lover!*

Kera

Yeah Dio's got a very big heart, but an even bigger temper
– *I blame the mother*

Nava (*rage*)

We're supposed to keep each other safe, ur evil you're destroying EVERYTHING!

Kera

Sorry you feel that way

The **Bacchae** *are divided. As* **Vida** *& her supporters retreat,* **Kera** *leads a War Cry.*

See, Vida hasn't got a fucking clue
How to worship our God but you
All know in Thebes Our God's a Native
So we shall take back his rightful Nation
Where you all claim your place to finally be safe in!
It's our first and final destination!
Women I know you're sick and tired
But Freedom's on the other side of One Last Riot

Bacchae

One Last Riot!

Kera

Agave – Our God's assembling you a feast
Hunter Queen, let's let you off your fucking leash!

Sixteen

En route to the mountain top, **Pentheus** *trips in a ditch.*

Pentheus

Ah, God, I think I need you to help me, we might have to . . . erm . . . hold hands

Dionysos

Or I could leave you to die and end this bromance

Pentheus (*in good humour*)
　Come on now

Dionysos
　Looking all vulnerable in this dress

Pentheus
　'Help someone help I'm a damsel in distress!'

They laugh, **Dionysos** *helps him out.*

　Careful though I don't want it to tear

Dionysos
　Relax bruv, why u so scared

Pentheus
　It *is* scary though . . . because
　Like, if, if I was a woman I think I'd feel very afraid

Dionysos (*surprised*)
　Oh. Yeah?

Pentheus
　I mean it's even scary sometimes just being a man

Dionysos
　Yeah fuckinell

Pentheus
　Fuckinell . . . yeah
　Everyone expects you can . . . expects you to . . .

Dionysos
　Yeah, they do, it's a lot of expecting to live up to

Pentheus
　And to protect women . . . is hard
　I've failed at that

Dionysos (*sarcastic*)
　Don't say that

Pentheus
　No I have, I've failed as a man . . . I've failed so badly as a man

That I'm dressed up as a woman to try & be the man I was meant to be
But I just want to feel like . . .

The words choke in his throat, he's about to burst, fighting tears away hard as he can but failing.

– just . . . I just . . . I just . . . miss *being a boy*
When I could be silly . . . or giddy whatever
It's just no one took notice or if they did they didn't take it serious

Pouring of him now, tears & snot the lot of it.

I used to paint my nails with my mum's nail varnish and they'd say oh he's being messy, like it wasn't judged, it didn't even mean anything cos I was a child and it wasn't *taken* to mean anything it was just, I didn't mean anything by it I was just being –

Dionysos
Free, I know

Pentheus
Lots of rules

Dionysos
Lots

Pentheus (*regaining composure*)
Lots lots lots
But now I've lost grip and I've . . . lost everyone
He's brainwashing my poor mother the woman who saved his life!

Dionysos
By turning him away?

Pentheus
She don't turn him away

Dionysos
You said she gave Dionysos up for adoption?

Pentheus
I know, I'm sorry, I was being cruel, I can get a bit spiky sometimes
That baby would never have been safe in Thebes.
She was protecting him from Hera's Fury

Dionysos
Reeeeewind – so wait wait
You're telling me Agave was protecting Dionysos from the start?

Pentheus
He's her *nephew* she couldn't help but have his best interests at heart

Dionysos
So she didn't reject him out of maliciousness it was the antithesis?

Pentheus
It's a . . . maternal instinct . . . woman-y . . . booby thing

Dionysos
Like a internal . . . womb-y fallopian tube-y thing!

Pentheus
But now he's turned into this vengeful attention seeking lost boy

Dionysos
So she didn't *turn* him away she . . . *sent* him away . . . to keep him safe?

Pentheus
You'd think he'd be grateful!

Dionysos
This is huge new information to drop at this point in the play, mate
Dionysos was hellbent on beheading u but now I guess his revenge is no longer credible

Pentheus
Obviously I've never met him but . . .
I don't get a friendly vibe from him to be honest?

Beat, sound of Bacchic singing in the near distance.

Dionysos
Hear that my cuz? We're close

Pentheus
We're close

Dionysos
We're very . . . *close*

Beat.

Pentheus
You 'cuz'?

Dionysos
Yeah . . . cuz
That – that's how men address each other where I'm from

Pentheus
Oh do they? (*Beat, bit giddy.*) I kinda like that *cuz* . . . the only nickname I ever had was Pen Pen, when I was a little boy my mum started calling me Pen Pen –

Dionysos
Shh listen

Pentheus (*whispers*)
The Bacchae

Dionysos
Okay cuz you see that Fir tree? Next to the Sycamore

Pentheus
Yes cuz I do cuz

Dionysos
Dionysos is gonna bend it down like a see-saw
And bring it here for
You

Pentheus
Literally bend that tree?

Dionysos
Think of it
As an Olive Branch

Pentheus
You can't be serious –

The tree magically bends in front of them ready for **Pentheus** *to sit on.*

Wow! Fuck me with a rubber ducky that is actually BENDING?!

Dionysos
What u thought I was pretending?

Pentheus
Nooo but it's cos like . . . *magic* . . . that means I'm cousins with an *actual God*God . . .?

Dionysos
Why u surprised? He's Zeus' son u said u already knew?

Pentheus
In truth we thought it made him just another bastard kid of Zeus
Not an actual God with real *God*God powers too?!

Pentheus *sits on tree and goes up.*

Ay Karumba

Dionysos
Steady, you're safe don't get fretty
It's all . . . good
See?

Pentheus
I'm flying in a tree, this has been the absolute craziest day ever

Pause, **Pentheus** *breathes it all in, in wonder and bliss.*

I can see them, wow, ah my mummy, oh my God she, (*squints*) she seems so . . . *happy?*

Dionysos

Cuz, how about, you think, like, there's any way we can avoid all this war?
Cos maybe you & Dionysos got more in common than you think
And you can like I dunno find common ground & discuss over a drink?

Pentheus

Cuz . . . that actually sounds . . . I think that's . . . *doable*

Dionysos

Doable!
Yes! It is isn't it?
Ur family after all, the only family I have, I mean *he* has left on earth, so it's worth a try right!

Pentheus

Ah I can't believe I'm saying this, I guess it is, yeah, *yeah*
And you know, I have to say, he owes a lot to you to be honest
I appreciate you trying so hard to help
You're not a bad guy . . . for a Bacchae!

Share a laugh, brings him down.

Dionysos

Dionysos thinks the same of you, he's impressed indeed
All he's ever wanted is to reunite the family in Thebes

Pentheus

Okay, listen, once Agave is home safe & sound
I'll agree to a Peace and . . . cuz, get ready to lose your shit

Dionysos

What what what?!

Pentheus
To Bacchae having land here in Thebes –

Dionysos
(*This is HUGE*)
Really? Woh! That is SO –

Pentheus
– in the mountains!

Dionysos
Oh . . .

Pentheus (*ecstatic*)
Side by side with real pure-blooded Thebans!

Dionysos
Mountains? In the margins?
What is your obsession with marginalisation?
I am never going back to being a Marginalised Asian.
Can't you find it in your heart to just properly let us in?

Pentheus
Let you in? What like *in* in?

Dionysos
Yeah *with* you!

Pentheus
With us? That's not possible
But, beside us, that's *doable*
I don't get the problem cuz it's a terrific offer, no?
That's *my* Olive Branch

Dionysos
Foreigners aren't tryna rob u blind & cause violence – that ain't why we seek asylum
Some of us just wanna blind u with lights, so cuz, prepare to be enlightened!

Vida *opens the wardrobe doors behind* **Dionysos**, *he is lit up by it,* **Dionysos** *summons stage lights to shine light on him, showing his true self to* **Pentheus**, *a shimmering God!*

Here *I* am.
Not a man
But a God!

Pentheus (*blinded by brightness*)
You're blinding me! It's too bright!

Dionysos
Dassright!

Pentheus
You – but that means you . . . you lied all this time?!

Dionysos
Duh!! This is the real me, no dress up, no pretend, a God who shares your blood, blud!

Pentheus
Shit I said so many blasphemous things to you, about you, to – to your face, holy shit!

Dionysos
Well, lucky you're my cousin!

Pentheus
But why, I don't get, why you didn't, just arrive like this in the first place?

Dionysos
I was . . . *scared*

Pentheus
Of what? You're a God!

Full with euphoric catharsis at FINALLY being able to be honest & authentic, emotion pours out.

Dionysos
Scared you'd reject me
Like Agave . . . or how I *thought* Agave . . . n I'd never recover

Pentheus
Instead of being honest you *kidnapped my mother*

Dionysos
Yes! But *this* – ah mate it's all I ever fucking wanted
I'm finally home, I can stop wondering the earth, we can
be together & rule together

Beat, looks like **Pentheus** *is convinced but then.*

Pentheus
I knew something like this would happen if I got sloppy!
Unite with you so women can abandon their children?
Queers can raise kids?! Over my dead body!
I'm in a fucking dress man!!!! How could I be so fucking
STUPID!

Dionysos
Cousin

Pentheus
Don't call me that you freak

Dionysos
Do not take my Benevolence for Weakness

Pentheus
You're a blackmailing thug, a foreign gangster not a God –

Dionysos
Why is it so hard for u to just worship a God?
I have made it as *simple* as *possible* for you to believe in me!

Pentheus
What kind of weak insecure God begs for a mortal's
worship?!

Dionysos
U won't worship me . . . *even to survive*? You'd rather die?

Pentheus
That's fucking right! I'd rather be eaten alive!

Dionysos
Stop faking! Drop the act!

Pentheus
Says you, the fakest real God there ever was!

Dionysos
Any mortal would feel honoured to be cousins with a God like me!

Pentheus
Not me! To me you'll always be Semele's lying, conniving *halfbreed mongrel!*

Dionysos
You just sealed your Fate.

Pentheus
No matter! Someone will take my place and hate you like I do
Your religion will be burnt to the ground
So do your worst, Mongrel, make me a Martyr!!

Dionysos *clicks his fingers,* **Bacchae** *appear,* **Dionysos** *exits as they surround* **Pentheus**.

Pentheus
Hey come back!
You Coward! Getting deranged women to do your dirty work for you?!

Agave *enters.*

Oh Mum! Mum hey!
What the fuck has he done to you?!
Please, mum, please! Mum!
It's Pentheus, it's your son!

Agave *when she's close enough pounces on her son and mauls him to death.*

Seventeen

The **Bacchae** *enter the Palace,* **Dionysos** *watches from above,* **Bacchae** *address audience.*

Demi
　Agave looked her son in his eyes

Serene
　Den she bit the vein right out his throat

Demi
　He woulda bled out n died from just the bite itself

Serene
　They didn't need to do nuttin else to him

Demi
　But they wanted to play with him, twisting him, ripping him
　Nibbling little chunks out of him

Nava
　Loadsa little chunks, his torso looked like Swiss cheese

Yunann
　Then they opened him up, like a flower blossoming

Serene
　It was fucking gnarly

Yunann
　It was a science experiment – human origami

Demi
　After they disembowelled him, they had a play with his skeleton

Yunann
　They stuck his arms n limbs behind his back
　Wrenched, levered and cracked
　Till every part of him snapped.

Demi
　Till every part of him . . . was apart from him

Kera
　We got very posh about it, didn't we girls?
　Assembled the pieces of him

Like how a fancy chef deconstructs a chicken
You know – the wing the leg the breast the thigh

Yunann
Except instead it was
The head the arm, the ankle the liver the heart

Kera
We've become so cultured
That we arranged his mural in town like a piece of
Modern Art
Then Agave screamed

Agave
Run like lightning!

Kera
To the palace I got a present for my –

Agave *enters holding* **Pentheus'** *decapitated head.*

Agave
Pentheus! I brought you a lion's head! A mountain lion!
Kera, my hunting tutor, how does my prowess impress
you?

Kera (*hint of regret*)
I didn't think you'd be so *impressionable*

Agave
It'll impress my Pentheus will it not? Oh my!

Kera
Sure majesty, if your boy could see that he'd die

Niloo
So you're happy yeah?

Agave
I'm delighted! And excited to show my Pentheus
Tell him Agave's caught an animal to make all the hunters
envious!

Sunny

Can I have the lion's teeth majesty? Dionysos really wants me to have em

Agave

Back off, he's my trophy you greedy madam

Tireseus (*enters*)

Agave, what have you done?!

Agave

Daddy come look I've brought a present for my son!

Tireseus

I'm not your –

Agave

Daddy look what I've carried here!
Scraped his head clean off with my bare hands didn't even have a spear
Pentheus is gonna lose his mind when he see's this!
Pass me a cup, I wanna see him drink it all up, my lion's thirsty!

Agave *pours the wine down* **Pentheus'** *mouth and it leaks out his decapitated throat.*

Now where on earth's my son? He better not be ignoring cos
I need teach him to be a good boy instead of warring Gods!

Tireseus

I need you to –

Agave

Now where on earth's my son? He better not be ignoring cos
I need teach him to be a good boy instead of warring Gods!

Tireseus
Look at your hands and try to truly see
Can you do that for me?

Agave
Okay . . . What is this? What is this?!
Surprise! Lion head!

Tireseus
Look into his eyes

Agave
His eyes?
His eyes . . . look alive
He stares at us

Tireseus
Do you know his name?

Agave
This . . . is Pentheus
This is
Pain

Tireseus
Now you know

Agave
Who killed Pentheus and put him in my hands?

Kera
This bitch is faking, I know she understands

Tireseus
You did

Agave
That's
Really
Stupid
Where did I do it?

Tireseus
In the cold air
Of the mountains

Agave
Why would Pentheus go there?

Tireseus
To save you

Agave
Why was I there?

Tireseus
You were Bacchae too

Agave
What have I done
My only son

Kera
Freedom has a cost but majesty, you were fearless

Agave
I thought he was a lion

Kera (*refusing to admit she's wrong*)
Well-behaved women don't make history

Agave
Trickery! We've all been driven insane by *him* all of us women
What are you all doing . . .?!

Vida
I don't even know no more. (*To* **Kera**.) Happy with what u done?

Kera
Na let's keep going, Bacchae dominion has just begun
Look at him looking so devious
Let's kill Tireseus

Tireseus
>I wonder, young lady, if you've paid attention as such
>But I can see into the future and I don't get killed thank you very much
>But as for you, if you find yourself in a storm 7 months from now, be wary of falling pine trees . . .

Dionysos, *horrified, enters the palace.*

Agave
>Hello nephew, you're awfully quiet for once
>Oh you cried so loudly in Zeus' arms
>I saved you when you were a baby boy
>Innocent Beautiful Baby Boy
>I told Zeus to keep you away from here
>So you could *live*
>I protected you
>Because that's what family do
>And in return you've destroyed us
>Your might be half God but the other half is definitely not human
>You don't deserve . . . *us*

Agave *exits.*

Dionysos
>Vida, what do I do?

Vida
>Live. Live with what u done son

Demi
>I am officially retiring my clipboard . . . I signed up for the God of a good time, man!
>Liberate a little bit, lick a clit, take a sip but *dis* . . . It ain't the Promised Land

Serene
>Why didn't u stop it fam? I was so sure u was gonna stop it

Dionysos
I thought . . . he was gonna . . . we got so close . . . I wanted him to just . . .

Serene
Why?

Dionysos
Cos – cos we're meant to be . . .

Vida
But *why*, son?

Dionysos
Maybe there's a difference between *being* a God and *feeling* like one
In fact, u know what, fuck being a God!

Nava
What?!
Thebes was a big mistake

Demi
Was it?

Kera
Why did u bring us here then??

Dionysos
I don't know. You shouldn't follow someone like me

Vida
Perhaps there was always a flaw in our plan
The Liberation of Women . . . being led by a man

Dionysos
I was supposed to use my Godly powers to make things properly actually better for u all but instead –

Vida
No God got the power to do that, bigheaded of u to think u would

Ignorant of us to think you could
Maybe it's finally time let go of your rage, aight?

Dionysos (*to audience*)
Pentheus is right, I am a Fake God
Even when I shimmer it's Fake Bright!
Zeus is the shining God of Lightning but I'm the flippin
. . . God of Stage Lights

Olympus grumbles above, opens its doors, floods blinding bright light on all, who are stunned.

Serene
Yo

Demi
What on earth?!

Vida
Das not on earth

Dionysos
What?! Olympus wants me as a God . . . of *Theatre*? My flippin side hustle?!

Serene
Aphrodite got Sexing, Ares got War, Athena got Wisdom – u got Theatre bruv that's some nerdy power even Demi could be the God of that

Vida
It makes sense

Serene
God of Theatre still don't make all dis right fam

Dionysos
You're right fam, but it does mean I can bring Pentheus back to life every night fam

Serene
That's beautiful fam I'm convinced fam

Demi
> But technically every night he'd still die so, so it'll still end like this every time?

Serene
> Why do u hate fun fam just try n not be a nerd for once in ur life!

Dionysos
> They want me right after I've proven I'm not worthy of being a God or a human?

Vida
> Yeah, mortals go thru some real shit son, who else gonna tell our fucked-up Fates
> You, you're the only God that could ever relate!

Serene
> Dio what if the Gods are pranking us fam dis could be a pisstake?

Vida
> It ain't. So take it. Now go sign out in style son, I raised a showman!

Dionysos
> Okay, Mummy Vida, as I'm officially the God of Theatre I'll do this
> *For all of us:* Whether you're an aristocrat or commoner

Serene
> Tonight the Artful Dodgers have taken over the Oliver!

Dionysos
> A place where we can tell real messed-up, effed-up stories
> Without gettin Stage Fright
> BTW – My name is Dionysos not die-oh-nigh-sis I might run up in ur local theatre for a Stage Fight If u don't start pronouncing my name right!

Tireseus
> I always have, but no one listens to me . . . about anything

Vida (*to audience*)
  What my son's tryna say is that the guard is now changing
  Ur theatre might have a King but we got a God as *our* patron!

Dionysos
  The underdogs are off their leashes n barking fam
  A half-God ain't *sub*human, street slang ain't *sub*culture dis language is *art*isan.

Vida (*bursting with pride & pain*)
  My son about to fly to Olympus . . . boy talk that shit!!

Dionysos
  I led us astray but we're gonna show them Gods we're modern-day Prometheans!

Vida
  I said – talk dat shit!!!

Dionysos
  Usain Bolt is gonna sprint to this stage to know what it feels like to meet a Real Olympian!

Dionysos *ascends to Olympus.*

Serene
  That's some Ancient Greek superhero shit

Vida
  The Prophecy said I'd lose my boy in his motherland
  But on the other hand, my loss is your gain
  After the God of Drama steps in ur Royal National Theatre shit'll never be the same
  You saw Agave's heartbreak, Pentheus' head snap
  If u saw Hope glimmer in the darkness, don't never forget *dat*
  Now the Stage is all yours, we just came to set the scene
  So get on your Spiderman shit – 'with great power comes great responsibility'
  And me? I merely create the spell pull the rabbit out the magic hat

Anansi, Houdini, Hubble Bubble Toil & Trouble dat
I go Hocus Pocus, *supercalifragilisticexpialidocious* &
Alakazam!
Then I disa-fucking-ppear like it never fucking happened
fam!

Vida *disappears, like magic.*

The End.

Discover. Read. Listen. Watch.

A NEW WAY TO ENGAGE WITH PLAYS

This award-winning digital library features over 3,000 playtexts, 400 audio plays, 300 hours of video and 360 scholarly books.

Playtexts published by Methuen Drama, The Arden Shakespeare, Faber & Faber, Playwrights Canada Press, Aurora Metro Books and Nick Hern Books.

Audio Plays from L.A. Theatre Works featuring classic and modern works from the oeuvres of leading American playwrights.

Video collections including films of live performances from the RSC, The Globe and The National Theatre, as well as acting masterclasses and BBC feature films and documentaries.

FIND OUT MORE:
www.dramaonlinelibrary.com • @dramaonlinelib

Methuen Drama Contemporary Dramatists

include

John Arden (two volumes)
Arden & D'Arcy
Peter Barnes (three volumes)
Sebastian Barry
Mike Bartlett
Clare Barron
Brad Birch
Dermot Bolger
Edward Bond (ten volumes)
Howard Brenton (two volumes)
Leo Butler (two volumes)
Richard Cameron
Jim Cartwright
Caryl Churchill (two volumes)
Complicite
Sarah Daniels (two volumes)
Nick Darke
David Edgar (three volumes)
David Eldridge (two volumes)
Ben Elton
Per Olov Enquist
Dario Fo (two volumes)
Michael Frayn (four volumes)
John Godber (four volumes)
Paul Godfrey
James Graham (two volumes)
David Greig
John Guare
Lee Hall (two volumes)
Katori Hall
Peter Handke
Jonathan Harvey (two volumes)
Iain Heggie
Israel Horovitz
Declan Hughes
Terry Johnson (three volumes)
Sarah Kane
Barrie Keeffe
Bernard-Marie Koltès (two volumes)
Franz Xaver Kroetz
Kwame Kwei-Armah
David Lan
Bryony Lavery
Deborah Levy
Doug Lucie
Alistair MacDowall
Sabrina Mahfouz
David Mamet (six volumes)
Patrick Marber
Martin McDonagh
Duncan McLean
David Mercer (two volumes)
Anthony Minghella (two volumes)
Rory Mullarkey
Tom Murphy (six volumes)
Phyllis Nagy
Anthony Neilson (three volumes)
Peter Nichol (two volumes)
Philip Osment
Gary Owen
Louise Page
Stewart Parker (two volumes)
Joe Penhall (two volumes)
Stephen Poliakoff (three volumes)
David Rabe (two volumes)
Mark Ravenhill (three volumes)
Christina Reid
Philip Ridley (two volumes)
Willy Russell
Eric-Emmanuel Schmitt
Ntozake Shange
Sam Shepard (two volumes)
Martin Sherman (two volumes)
Christopher Shinn (two volumes)
Joshua Sobel
Wole Soyinka (two volumes)
Simon Stephens (five volumes)
Shelagh Stephenson
David Storey (three volumes)
C. P. Taylor
Sue Townsend
Judy Upton (two volumes)
Michel Vinaver (two volumes)
Arnold Wesker (two volumes)
Peter Whelan
Michael Wilcox
Roy Williams (four volumes)
David Williamson
Snoo Wilson (two volumes)
David Wood (two volumes)
Victoria Wood

Methuen Drama Modern Plays

include

Bola Agbaje
Ayad Akhtar
Edward Albee
Jean Anouilh
John Arden
Peter Barnes
Clare Barron
Sebastian Barry
Alistair Beaton
Brendan Behan
Edward Bond
William Boyd
Bertolt Brecht
Howard Brenton
Amelia Bullmore
Anthony Burgess
Leo Butler
Jim Cartwright
Lolita Chakrabarti
Caryl Churchill
Lucinda Coxon
Tim Crouch
Shelagh Delaney
Ishy Din
Claire Dowie
David Edgar
David Eldridge
Dario Fo
Michael Frayn
John Godber
James Graham
David Greig
John Guare
Lauren Gunderson
Peter Handke
David Harrower
Jonathan Harvey
Robert Holman
David Ireland
Sarah Kane
Barrie Keeffe
Jasmine Lee-Jones
Anders Lustgarten
Duncan Macmillan
David Mamet
Patrick Marber
Martin McDonagh
Alistair McDowall
Arthur Miller
Tom Murphy
Phyllis Nagy
Anthony Neilson
Peter Nichols
Ben Okri
Joe Orton
Vinay Patel
Joe Penhall
Luigi Pirandello
Stephen Poliakoff
Lucy Prebble
Peter Quilter
Mark Ravenhill
Philip Ridley
Willy Russell
Sam Shepard
Martin Sherman
Chris Shinn
Jackie Sibblies Drury
Wole Soyinka
Simon Stephens
Kae Tempest
Laura Wade
Anne Washburn
Timberlake Wertenbaker
Roy Williams
Snoo Wilson
Theatre Workshop
Frances Ya-Chu Cowhig
Benjamin Zephaniah

Methuen Drama Student Editions

Alan Ayckbourn *Confusions* • **Mike Bartlett** *Earthquakes in London* • **Aphra Behn** *The Rover* • **Alice Birch** *Revolt. She Said. Revolt Again* • **Edward Bond** *Lear* • *Saved* • **Bertolt Brecht** *The Caucasian Chalk Circle* • *Fear and Misery in the Third Reich* • *The Good Person of Szechwan* • *Life of Galileo* • *Mother Courage and her Children* • *The Resistible Rise of Arturo Ui* • *The Threepenny Opera* • **Jon Brittain** *Rotterdam* • **Georg Büchner** *Woyzeck* • **Anton Chekhov** *The Cherry Orchard* • *The Seagull* • *Three Sisters* • *Uncle Vanya* • **Caryl Churchill** *Serious Money* • *Top Girls* • **Shelagh Delaney** *A Taste of Honey* • **Inua Ellams** *Barber Shop Chronicles* • **Euripides** *Elektra* • *Medea* • **Dario Fo** *Accidental Death of an Anarchist* • **Michael Frayn** *Copenhagen* • **John Galsworthy** *Strife* • **Nikolai Gogol** *The Government Inspector* • **Carlo Goldoni** *A Servant to Two Masters* • **James Graham** *This House* • **Tanika Gupta** *The Empress* • **Katori Hall** *The Mountaintop* • **Lorraine Hansberry** *A Raisin in the Sun* • **Robert Holman** *Across Oka* • **Henrik Ibsen** *A Doll's House* • *Ghosts* • *Hedda Gabler* • **Sarah Kane** *4.48 Psychosis* • *Blasted* • **Charlotte Keatley** *My Mother Said I Never Should* • **Dennis Kelly** *DNA* • **Bernard Kops** *Dreams of Anne Frank* • **Federico García Lorca** *Blood Wedding* • *Doña Rosita the Spinster* (bilingual edition) • *The House of Bernarda Alba* (bilingual edition) • *Yerma* (bilingual edition) • **David Mamet** *Glengarry Glen Ross* • *Oleanna* • **Patrick Marber** *Closer* • **John Marston** *The Malcontent* • **Martin McDonagh** *The Lieutenant of Inishmore* • *The Lonesome West* • *The Beauty Queen of Leenane* • *The Cripple of Inishmaan* • **Alistair McDowall** *Pomona* • **John McGrath** *The Cheviot, the Stag and the Black, Black Oil* • **Arthur Miller** *All My Sons* • *The Crucible* • *A View from the Bridge* • *Death of a Salesman* • *The Price* • *After the Fall* • *The Last Yankee* • *A Memory of Two Mondays* • *Broken Glass* • *Incident at Vichy* • *The American Clock* • *The Ride Down Mt. Morgan* • **Joe Orton** *Loot* • **Joe Penhall** *Blue/Orange* • **Luigi Pirandello** *Six Characters in Search of an Author* • **Lucy Prebble** *Enron* • **Mark Ravenhill** *Shopping and F***ing* • **Reginald Rose** *Twelve Angry Men* • **Willy Russell** *Blood Brothers* • *Educating Rita* • **Lemn Sissay** Benjamin Zephaniah's *Refugee Boy* • **Sophocles** *Antigone* • *Oedipus the King* • **Wole Soyinka** *Death and the King's Horseman* • **Simon Stephens** *Punk Rock* • *Pornography* • **Shelagh Stephenson** *The Memory of Water* • **August Strindberg** *Miss Julie* • **J. M. Synge** *The Playboy of the Western World* • **Kae Tempest** *Wasted* • **Theatre Workshop** *Oh What a Lovely War* • **Laura Wade** *Posh* • **Frank Wedekind** *Spring Awakening* • **Timberlake Wertenbaker** *Our Country's Good* • **Arnold Wesker** *The Merchant* • **Peter Whelan** *The Accrington Pals* • **Oscar Wilde** *The Importance of Being Earnest* • **Roy Williams** *Sing Yer Heart Out for the Lads* • **Tennessee Williams** *A Streetcar Named Desire* • *The Glass Menagerie* • *Cat on a Hot Tin Roof* • *Sweet Bird of Youth*

For a complete listing of
Methuen Drama titles, visit:
www.bloomsbury.com/drama

Follow us on X and keep up to date with
our news and publications
@MethuenDrama

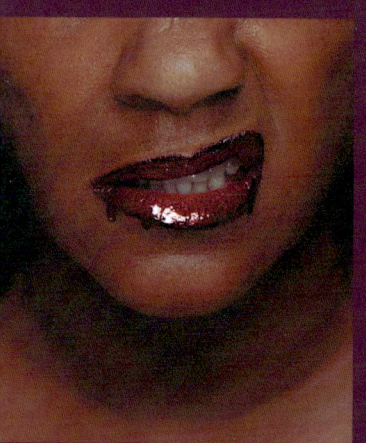

This ain't no classic play.

The Bacchae aren't standing on the sidelines whilst the men have all the fun. These fangirls may be a pack but they're not animals… They are stage-storming powerhouses ready to cause chaos in Thebes.

Whilst the Bacchae maraud in the mountains, their god Dionysos is taking part in his own f*cked-up family Olympics. He's here to bring down his cousin King Pentheus. All to prove to the chorus of women that he's more than just the god of rhyme, wine and a good time.

The first ever playwright debut on the National Theatre's Olivier stage, Nima Taleghani's exciting new version of Euripides' ultimate tragedy is brought to life through rhythm, movement and music.

This edition was published to coincide with the world premiere production in September 2025, directed by Director of the National Theatre Indhu Rubasingham.